WHEN
CHRIST COMES

WHEN CHRIST COMES

THE BEGINNING OF THE VERY BEST

MAX LUCADO

THOMAS NELSON
Since 1798

NASHVILLE   DALLAS   MEXICO CITY   RIO DE JANEIRO

Unless otherwise noted, Scripture quotations are from New Century Version®. © 2005 by Thomas Nelson. Used by permission. All rights reserved.

Other Scripture references are from the following sources:

THE CONTEMPORARY ENGLISH VERSION (CEV). © 1991 by the American Bible Society. Used by permission. *The Living Bible* (TLB). © 1971. Used by permission of Tyndale House Publishers, Inc., Wheaton, Illinois 60189. *The Message* by Eugene H. Peterson (MSG). © 1993. Used by permission of NavPress Publishing Group. All rights reserved. THE NEW KING JAMES VERSION (NKJV). © 1982 by Thomas Nelson. Used by permission. All rights reserved. J. B. Phillips: THE NEW TESTAMENT IN MODERN ENGLISH, Revised Edition (PHILLIPS). © J. B. Phillips 1958, 1960, 1972. Used by permission of Macmillan Publishing Co., Inc. NEW AMERICAN STANDARD BIBLE® (NASB), © The Lockman Foundation 1960, 1962, 1963, 1968, 1971, 1972, 1973, 1975, 1977. Used by permission. REVISED STANDARD VERSION of the Bible (RSV). © 1946, 1952, 1971, 1973 by the Division of Christian Education of the National Council of the Churches of Christ in the U.S.A. Used by permission. THE JERUSALEM BIBLE (JB). © 1966 by Darton, Longman & Todd Ltd. and Doubleday & Company, Inc. Used by permission. NEW REVISED STANDARD VERSION of the Bible (NRSV). © 1989 by the Division of Christian Education of the National Council of the Churches of Christ in the U.S.A. All rights reserved. Today's English Version (TEV). © American Bible Society 1966, 1971, 1976. The Holy Bible, New International Version®, (NIV). Copyright © 1973, 1978, 1984 by Biblica, Inc.™ Used by permission of Zondervan. All rights reserved worldwide. *www.zondervan.com.* THE NEW ENGLISH BIBLE. © 1961, 1970 by The Delegates of the Oxford University Press and the Syndics of the Cambridge University Press. Reprinted by permission. *Holy Bible*, New Living Translation (NLT). © 1996. Used by permission of Tyndale House Publishers, Inc., Wheaton, Illinois 60189. All rights reserved.

ISBN 978-0-8499-4297-6 (tp)
ISBN 978-0-8499-6443-5 (repack)

Library of Congress Cataloging-in-Publication Data

Lucado, Max.
When Christ comes / Max Lucado.
p. cm.
ISBN 0-8499-1298-9 (hc)
ISBN 0-8499-3783-3 (international)
ISBN 978-0-8499-6443-5 (repackage)
1. Second Advent. I. Title.
BT886.L79 1999
236'.9—dc21   99-30283
CIPP

Printed in the United States of America

13 14 15 16 17 RRD 6 5 4 3 2 1

To my mother
Thelma Lucado
You gave more than birth—you gave yourself.
And I love you.

CONTENTS

   Thoughts of the Second Coming unsettle me. Life
   with no end? Space with no bounds? And what about
   Armageddon, the lake of fire, the mark of the beast?
   Am I supposed to understand all this? Am I supposed
   to feel good about all this?

   Some Christians are so obsessed with the last days that
   they are oblivious to these days. Others are just the
   opposite. They'll tell you Jesus is coming. But they

live like he never will. One is too panicky, the other too
patient. Isn't there a balance?

A Day of Proof and Promise

I'm the cautious type. I want to believe in Jesus' promise
to return, but can I? Dare I trust the words of a small-
town carpenter spoken two thousand years ago in a remote
nation? Can I really believe in what Jesus says about his
coming?

A Day of Happy Reunions

What about my loved ones who have died? Where are
they now? In the time between our death and Christ's
return, what happens?

A Day of Rejuvenation

What's all this talk about a new body? Do we change
bodies? Is the new one different than this one? Will I
recognize anyone? Will anyone recognize me?

A Day of Redemption

There I am, at the entryway to heaven. My family enters,
my friends enter, but when my turn comes, the door is
closed. How can I know I won't be turned away?

Contents

ACKNOWLEDGMENTS

YEARS AGO I HEARD A CUTE, LIKELY APOCRYPHAL STORY about Mark Twain. A Sunday school teacher told the author that his name had surfaced in Bible class. One of her young students was attempting to quote the names of the books in the New Testament. He began by saying, "Matthew, Mark Twain, Luke, and John."

"What do you think of that, Mr. Twain?" she inquired.

"Well," he replied, "it's been a long time since I've been in finer company."

I can say the same. Through the course of writing this book, I've enjoyed the company of some of God's finest children. And to a few of them, I offer a word of gratitude.

To my editor, Liz Heaney—How many books have we done now? More than a dozen, right? Each one hopefully better than the one before. Each one certainly more fun than the one before. Thanks for being such a friend and not chuckling too loud at my mistakes.

To my assistant, Karen Hill—Somehow you do it all. Run the office. Run interference. Run to my aid when I'm in trouble. But, in the process, you never run out of laughter or energy. You are one of a kind. Thank you so, so, so much.

To Steve and Cheryl Green, Austin, Caroline, and Claire—As sure as the sun shines and sets, you are faithful friends. Thanks for being Jesus to our family.

To Steve Halliday—Thanks for another thoughtful study guide that stretches the mind and challenges the heart.

To the Thomas Nelson family—No author could entrust himself to a finer team.

To the Oak Hills congregation—What a year it has been! New location. New facility. New schedule. I'm so glad you didn't opt for a new preacher. We live in a time of answered prayer. For the privilege of sharing God's Word with you each week, I am eternally grateful.

To the Oak Hills elders—For your diligent pastoral care of the church, for your brotherly love for my family, for your ceaseless prayers for my work, I thank you.

To the (growing) Oak Hills staff—You are the finest, and I'm proud to be on the team.

To Victor and Tara McCracken—Thanks for a summer full of study. Welcome to San Antonio.

To Becky Rayburn, our office angel—What a blessing you are!

To my daughters, Jenna, Andrea, and Sara—One in high

school, one in middle school, and one in elementary school, but all in my heart. I love you dearly.

And to my wife, Denalyn—To show me his grace, God gave me the cross. To show me his extravagance, God gave me you.

And to you, the reader—As your guide for the next few pages, I'll do my best to do my job: speaking up when I have something to offer and shutting up when I don't. And at any point, if you feel like closing the book and chatting with the real Author, please do.

I'll still be here when you return.

WHEN CHRIST COMES

You are in your car driving home. Thoughts wander to the game you want to see or meal you want to eat, when suddenly a sound unlike any you've ever heard fills the air. The sound is high above you. A trumpet? A choir? A choir of trumpets? You don't know, but you want to know. So you pull over, get out of your car, and look up. As you do, you see you aren't the only curious one. The roadside has become a parking lot. Car doors are open, and people are staring at the sky. Shoppers are racing out of the grocery store. The Little League baseball game across the street has come to a halt. Players and parents are searching the clouds.

And what they see, and what you see, has never before been seen.

As if the sky were a curtain, the drapes of the atmosphere part. A brilliant light spills onto the earth. There are no shadows. None. From whence came the light begins to tumble a river of color—spiking crystals of every hue ever seen and a million more never seen. Riding on the flow is an endless fleet of angels. They pass through the curtains one myriad at a time, until they occupy every square inch of the sky. North. South. East. West. Thousands of silvery wings rise and fall in unison, and over the sound of the trumpets, you can hear the cherubim and seraphim chanting, "Holy, holy, holy."

The final flank of angels is followed by twenty-four silver-bearded elders and a multitude of souls who join the angels in worship. Presently the movement stops and the trumpets are silent, leaving only the trium-phant triplet: "Holy, holy, holy." Between each word is a pause. With each word, a profound reverence. You hear your voice join in the chorus. You don't know why you say the words, but you know you must.

Suddenly, the heavens are quiet. All is quiet. The angels turn, you turn, the entire world turns—and there he is. Jesus. Through waves of light you see the silhouetted figure of Christ the King. He is atop a great stallion, and the stallion is atop a billowing cloud. He opens his mouth, and you are surrounded by his declaration: "I am the Alpha and the Omega."

The angels bow their heads. The elders remove their crowns. And before you is a figure so consuming that you know, instantly you know: Nothing else matters. Forget stock markets and school reports. Sales meetings and football games. Nothing is newsworthy. All that mattered, matters no more, for Christ has come . . .

〜◦〜

I wonder how those words make you feel. Wouldn't it be interesting to sit in a circle and listen to people's reactions? If a cluster of us summarized our emotions regarding the return of Christ in one word—what words would we hear? What word would you use?

Discomfort? Likely a popular choice. You've been told your mistakes will be revealed. You've been told your secrets will be made known. Books will be opened, and names will be read. You know God is holy. You know you are not. How could the thought of his return bring anything but discomfort?

Besides, there are all those phrases—"the mark of the beast," "the Antichrist," and "the battle of Armageddon." And what about "the wars and rumors of wars"? And what was that the fellow said on TV? "Avoid all phone numbers with the digits 666." And that magazine article disclosing the new senator as the Antichrist? Discomforting, to say the least.

Or perhaps discomfort is not your word of choice. *Denial* might be more accurate. (Or maybe it's by denial that you deal with the discomfort?) Ambiguity is not a pleasant roommate. We prefer answers and explanations, and the end of time seems short on both. Consequently, you opt not to think about it. Why consider what you can't explain? If he comes, fine. If not, fine. But I'm going to bed. I have to work tomorrow.

Or how about this word—*disappointment?* This one may surprise you, unless you've felt it; then you'll relate. Who would feel disappointment at the thought of Christ's coming? A mother-to-be might—she wants to hold her baby. An engaged couple might—they want to be married. A soldier stationed overseas might—he wants to go home before he goes home.

This trio is just a sampling of the many emotions stirred by the thought of Christ's return. Others might be *obsessed*. (These are the folks with the charts and codes and you-better-believe-it prophecies.) *Panic*. ("Sell everything and head to the hills!")

I wonder what God would want us to feel. It's not hard to find the answer. Jesus said it plainly in John 14: "Don't let your hearts be troubled. Trust in God, and trust in me. . . . I will come back and take you to be with me" (vv. 1, 3). It's a simple scenario. The Father has gone away for a while. But he will return. And until then, he wants his children to be at peace.

I want the same for my three daughters.

I left them last night so I could get away and finish this book. With a kiss and a hug, I walked out the door and promised to return. Did I want to leave them? No. But this book needed some work, and the publisher needed a manuscript, so here I am—in a hideaway—pounding a computer keyboard. We have accepted the fact that a time of separation is necessary to finish the job.

While we are apart, do I want them to feel discomfort? Do I want them dreading my return? No.

What about denial? Would I be pleased to hear that they have removed my picture from the mantel and my plate from the table and are refusing to discuss my arrival? I don't think so.

How about disappointment? "Oh, I hope Daddy doesn't come

before Friday night—I really want to go to that slumber party." Am I such a fuddy-dud dad that my coming will spoil the fun?

Well, perhaps I am. But God isn't. And, if he has his way with us, thoughts of his return won't disappoint his children. He, too, is away from his family. He, too, has promised to return. He isn't writing a book, but he is writing history. My daughters don't understand all the intricacies of my task; we don't understand all the details of his. But our job in the meantime? Trust. Soon the final chapter will be crafted and he'll appear at the door. But until then Jesus says: "Don't let your hearts be troubled. Trust in God, and trust in me."

This is the desire of God. It's also the aim of this book.

No book can answer all the questions. And no reader will agree with all my suggestions. (Some of you were only a few lines into the opening description of the return before you stubbed an opinion on a sentence.) But perhaps God will use this book to encourage you to be at peace about his coming.

Would you like to discuss the end of time and feel better because of it? Could you use some comforting words regarding the return of Christ? If so, I think I've found some.

Let's talk.

One

"You Do the Trusting; I'll Do the Taking"

When Will He Come?

Don't let your hearts be troubled. Trust in God, and trust in me.
. . . I will come back and take you to be with me.

JOHN 14:1, 3

PARENTING IS PACKED WITH CHALLENGES. WHO AMONG us has answers to the questions children ask?

"Why can't I have another puppy?"

"But you got married when you were eighteen. Why can't I?"

"Daddy, what is Viagra?"

Such questions would cause a sage to stammer. They pale, however, compared to one a child asks on a trip. In a comprehensive survey conducted by Lucado and Friends (I interviewed a couple of people in the hallway), I determined the most dreaded question in parentdom. What is the single query hated most by moms and dads? It's the one posed by the five-year-old on the trip, "How much farther?"

———

Give us the dilemmas of geometry and sexuality; just don't make a parent answer the question, "How much farther?"

It's an impossible question. How do you speak of time and distance to someone who doesn't understand time and distance? The novice parent assumes the facts will suffice, "Two hundred and fifty miles." But what do miles mean to a pre-K kid? Nothing! You might as well have spoken Yiddish! So the child asks, "What is two hundred and fifty miles?" At this point you're tempted to get technical and explain that one mile equals 5,280 feet, so two hundred and fifty miles equals one million three hundred thousand feet. But four words into the sentence, and the child tunes you out. He sits quietly until you are quiet and then asks, "How much farther?"

The world of a youngster is delightfully free of mile markers and alarm clocks. You can speak of minutes and kilometers, but a child has no hooks for those hats. So what do you do? Most parents get creative. When our girls were toddlers, they loved to watch *The Little Mermaid*. So Denalyn and I used the movie as an economy of scale. "About as long as it takes you to watch *The Little Mermaid* three times."

And for a few minutes that seemed to help. But sooner or later, they ask again. And sooner or later, we say what all parents eventually say, "Just trust me. You enjoy the trip and don't worry about the details. I'll make sure we get home OK."

And we mean it. We don't want our kids to sweat the details. So we make a deal with them, "We'll do the taking. You do the trusting."

Sound familiar? It might. Jesus has said the same to us. Just prior to his crucifixion, he told his disciples that he would be leaving them. "Where I am going you cannot follow now, but you will follow later" (John 13:36).

Such a statement was bound to stir some questions. Peter spoke for the others and asked, "Lord, why can't I follow you now?" (v. 37).

See if Jesus' reply doesn't reflect the tenderness of a parent to a child: "Don't let your hearts be troubled. Trust in God, and trust in me. There are many rooms in my Father's house; I would not tell you this if it were not true. I am going there to prepare a place for you. . . . I will come back and take you to be with me so that you may be where I am going" (John 14:1–3).

Reduce the paragraph to a sentence and it might read: "You do the trusting and I'll do the taking." A healthy reminder when it comes to anticipating the return of Christ. For many, the verb *trust* is not easily associated with his coming.

Our pre-K minds are ill-equipped to handle the thoughts of eternity. When it comes to a world with no boundaries of space and time, we don't have the hooks for those hats. Consequently, our Lord takes the posture of a parent, "You do the trusting and I'll do the taking." This is precisely his message in these warm words of John 14. Let's ponder them for a bit.

All of his words can be reduced to two: *Trust me.* "Don't let your hearts be troubled. Trust in God, and trust in me" (v. 1).

Don't be troubled by the return of Christ. Don't be anxious

about things you cannot comprehend. Issues like the millennium and the Antichrist are intended to challenge and stretch us, but not overwhelm and certainly not divide us. For the Christian, the return of Christ is not a riddle to be solved or a code to be broken, but rather a day to be anticipated.

Jesus wants us to trust him. He doesn't want us to be troubled, so he reassures us with these truths.

I have ample space for you. "There are many rooms in my Father's house" (v. 2). Why does Jesus refer to "many rooms"? Why does our Master make a point of mentioning the size of the house? You can answer that question as you think of the many times in life you've heard the opposite. Haven't there been occasions when you've been told: "We have no room for you here"?

Have you heard it in the workplace? "Sorry, I don't have room for you in my business."

Have you heard it in sports? "We don't have room for you on this team."

From someone you love? "I don't have room for you in my heart."

From a bigot? "We don't have room for your type in here."

Most sadly, have you heard it from a church? "You've made too many mistakes. We don't have room for you here."

Some of the saddest words on earth are: "We don't have room for you."

Jesus knew the sound of those words. He was still in Mary's womb when the innkeeper said, "We don't have room for you."

When the residents of his hometown tried to stone him, were they not saying the same? "We don't have room for prophets in this town."

When the religious leaders accused him of blasphemy, weren't they shunning him? "We don't have room for a self-proclaimed Messiah in this country."

And when he was hung on the cross, wasn't the message one of utter rejection? "We don't have room for you in this world."

Even today Jesus is given the same treatment. He goes from heart to heart, asking if he might enter. But more often than not, he hears the words of the Bethlehem innkeeper: "Sorry. Too crowded. I don't have room for you here."

But every so often, he is welcomed. Someone throws open the door of his or her heart and invites him to stay. And to that person Jesus gives this great promise: "Do not let your heart be troubled. Trust in God. And trust in me. In my Father's house are many rooms."

"I have ample space for you," he says. What a delightful promise he makes us! We make room for him in our hearts, and he makes room for us in his house. His house has ample space.

His house has a second blessing:

I have a prepared place for you. "I am going there to prepare a place for you" (v. 2). A few years back I spent a week speaking at a church in California. The members of the congregation were incredible hosts and hostesses. All my meals were lined up, each at a different house, each house with a full table

7

and at each table wonderful conversation. But after a few meals, I noticed something strange. All we ate was salad. I like salad as much as the next guy, but I prefer it as a warmup to the main act. But everywhere I went, it was the main act. No meat. No dessert. Just salads.

At first I thought it was a California thing. But finally I had to ask. The answer confused me. "We were told that you eat nothing but salads." Well, I quickly corrected them, and wondered how they had heard such a preposterous distortion. As we traced the trail back, we determined that a miscommunication had occurred between our office and theirs.

The hosts meant well, but their information was bad. I'm happy to say that we corrected the problem and enjoyed some good meat. I'm even happier to say Jesus won't make the same mistake with you.

He is doing for you what my California friends did for me. He is preparing a place. There is a difference, however. He knows exactly what you need. You needn't worry about getting bored or tired or weary with seeing the same people or singing the same songs. And you certainly needn't worry about sitting down to meal after meal of salad.

He is preparing the perfect place for you. I love John MacArthur's definition of eternal life, "Heaven is the perfect place for people made perfect."[1]

Trust the promises of Christ. "I have ample space for you; I have a prepared place for you."

And one last commitment from Jesus:

I'm not kidding. "I will come back and take you to be with me so that you may be where I am going" (v. 3). Can you detect a slight shift of tone in the last verse? The first sentences are couched in warmth. "Don't be troubled." "Trust God." "There are many rooms." There is kindness in these words. But then the tone changes. Just slightly. The kindness continues but is now spiked with conviction. "I will come back. . . ."

George Tulloch displayed similar determination. In 1996 he led an expedition to the spot where the *Titanic* sank in 1912. He and his crew recovered numerous artifacts, everything from eyeglasses to jewelry to dishware. In his search, Tulloch realized that a large piece of the hull had broken from the ship and was resting not far from the vessel. Tulloch immediately saw the opportunity at hand. Here was a chance to rescue part of the ship itself.

The team set out to raise the twenty-ton piece of iron and place it onto the boat. They were successful in lifting it to the surface, but a storm blew in and the ropes broke and the Atlantic reclaimed her treasure. Tulloch was forced to retreat and regroup. But before he left, he did something curious. He descended into the deep and, with the robotic arm of his submarine, attached a strip of metal to a section of the hull. On the metal he'd written these words, "I will come back, George Tulloch."[2]

At first glance, his action is humorous. I mean, it's not like he has to worry about a lot of people stealing his piece of iron. For one thing, it's two and one-half miles below the surface of the

Atlantic. For another, well, it's a piece of junk. We wonder why anyone would be so attracted to it.

Of course, one might say the same about you and me. Why would God go to such efforts to reclaim us? What good are we to him? He must have his reasons because two thousand years ago, he entered the murky waters of our world in search of his children. And on all who will allow him to do so, he lays his claim and tags his name. "I will come back," he says.

George Tulloch did. Two years later he returned and rescued the piece of iron.

Jesus will as well. We don't know when he will come for us. We don't know how he will come for us. And, we really don't even know why he would come for us. Oh, we have our ideas and opinions. But most of what we have is faith. Faith that he has ample space and a prepared place and, at the right time, he will come so that we can be where he is.

He will do the taking. It's up to us to do the trusting.

Two

Waiting Forwardly

A Day to Anticipate

So what kind of people should you be? You should live holy lives and serve God, as you wait for and look forward to the coming of the day of God.

2 PETER 3:11–12

FUNNY HOW SCRIPTURE REMEMBERS DIFFERENT PEOPLE. Abraham is remembered trusting. Envision Moses, and you envision a person leading. Paul's place in Scripture was carved by his writing and John is known for his loving. But Simeon is remembered, interestingly enough, not for leading nor preaching nor loving, but rather for looking.

"Now in Jerusalem there was a man named Simeon. He was an upright and devout man; he *looked forward* to Israel's comforting and the Holy Spirit rested on him" (Luke 2:25 TJB, emphasis mine).

Let's take a look at Simeon, the man who knew how to wait

for the arrival of Christ. The way he waited for the first coming is a model for how we should wait for the Second Coming.

Our brief encounter with Simeon occurs eight days after the birth of Jesus. Joseph and Mary have brought their son to the temple. It's the day of a sacrifice, the day of circumcision, the day of dedication. But for Simeon, it's the day of celebration.

Let's imagine a white-headed, wizened fellow working his way down the streets of Jerusalem. People in the market call his name and he waves but doesn't stop. Neighbors greet him and he returns the greeting but doesn't pause. Friends chat on the corner and he smiles but doesn't stop. He has a place to be and he hasn't time to lose.

Verse 27 contains this curious statement: "Prompted by the Spirit he came to the Temple" (TJB). Simeon apparently had no plans to go to the temple. God, however, thought otherwise. We don't know how the prompting came—a call from a neighbor, an invitation from his wife, a nudging within the heart—we don't know. But somehow Simeon knew to clear his calendar and put away his golf clubs. "I think I'll go to church," he announced.

On this side of the event, we understand the prompting. Whether Simeon understood or not, we don't know. We do know, however, that this wasn't the first time God tapped him on the shoulder. At least one other time in his life, he had received a message from God.

"The Holy Spirit had revealed to him that he would not die until he had seen him—God's anointed King" (v. 26 TLB).

You've got to wonder what a message like that would do to a person. What does it do to you if you know you will someday see God? We know what it did to Simeon.

He was "constantly expecting the Messiah" (v. 25 TLB).

He was "living in expectation of the salvation of Israel" (v. 25 PHILLIPS).

He "watched and waited for the restoration of Israel" (v. 25 NEB).

Simeon is a man on tiptoe, wide-eyed and watching for the one who will come to save Israel.

Maybe you know what it's like to look for someone who has come for you. I do. When I travel somewhere to speak, I often don't know who will pick me up at the airport. Someone has been sent, but I don't know the person. Hence, I exit the plane searching the faces for a face I've never seen. But though I've never seen the person, I know I'll find him. He may have my name on a sign, or my book in his hand, or just a puzzled expression on his face. Were you to ask me how I will recognize the one who has come for me, I would say, "I don't know, I just know I will."

I bet Simeon would have said the same. "How will you know the king, Simeon?" "I don't know. I just know I will." And so he searches. Like Columbo after clues, he searches. Studying each passing face. Staring into the eyes of strangers. He's looking for someone.

The Greek language, rich as it is with terms, has a stable full of verbs which mean "to look." One means to "look up," another "look away;" one is used to "look upon" and another "looking in."

To "look at something intently" requires one word and to "look over someone carefully" mandates another.

Of all the forms of *look*, the one which best captures what it means to "look for the coming" is the term used to describe the action of Simeon: *prosdechomai*. *Dechomai* meaning "to wait." *Pros* meaning "forward." Combine them and you have the graphic picture of one "waiting forwardly." The grammar is poor, but the image is great. Simeon was waiting; not demanding, not hurrying, he was waiting.

At the same time, he was waiting *forwardly*. Patiently vigilant. Calmly expectant. Eyes open. Arms extended. Searching the crowd for the right face, and hoping the face appears today.

Such was the lifestyle of Simeon, and such can be ours. Haven't we, like Simeon, been told of the coming Christ? Aren't we, like Simeon, heirs of a promise? Are we not prompted by the same Spirit? Are we not longing to see the same face?

Absolutely. In fact, the very same verb is used later in Luke to describe the posture of the waiting servant:

> Be dressed, ready for service, and have your lamps shining. Be like servants who are waiting [*prosdechomai*] for their master to come home from a wedding party. When he comes and knocks, the servants immediately open the door for him. They will be blessed when their master comes home, because he sees that they were watching for him. I tell you the truth, the master will dress himself to serve and tell the servants to sit at the table, and he will serve them. (Luke 12:35–37)

Please note the posture of the servants: ready and waiting. Please note the action of the master. He is so thrilled that his attendants are watching for him that he takes the form of a servant and serves them! They sit at the feast and are cared for by the master! Why? Why are they honored in such a way? The master loves to find people looking for his return. The master rewards those who "wait forwardly."

Both words are crucial.

First, we must *wait*. Paul says "we are hoping for something we do not have yet, and we are waiting for it patiently" (Rom. 8:25). Simeon is our model. He was not so consumed with the "not yet" that he ignored the "right now." Luke says Simeon was a "good man and godly" (Luke 2:25). Peter urges us to follow suit.

"The day of the Lord will come like a thief. The skies will disappear with a loud noise. Everything in them will be destroyed by fire, and the earth and everything in it will be burned up. In that way everything will be destroyed. So what kind of people should you be?" (2 Peter 3:10–11).

Great question. What kind of people should we be? Peter tells us: "You should live holy lives and serve God, as you wait for and *[here is that word again]* look forward to the coming of the day of God" (vv. 11–12).

Hope of the future is not a license for irresponsibility in the present. Let us wait forwardly, but let us wait.

But for most of us, waiting is not our problem Or, maybe I should state, waiting *is* our problem. We are so good at waiting that we don't wait *forwardly*. We forget to look. We are so patient that we become complacent. We are too content. We seldom search the skies. We rarely run to the temple. We seldom, if ever, allow the Holy Spirit to interrupt our plans and lead us to worship so that we might see Jesus.

It is to those of us who are strong in waiting and weak in watching that our Lord was speaking when he said, "No one knows when that day or time will be, not the angels in heaven, not even the Son. Only the Father knows. . . . So always be ready, because you don't know the day your Lord will come. . . . The Son of Man will come at a time you don't expect him" (Matt. 24:36, 42, 44).

Simeon reminds us to "wait forwardly." Patiently vigilant. But not so patient that we lose our vigilance. Nor so vigilant that we lose our patience.

In the end, the prayer of Simeon was answered. "Simeon took the baby in his arms and thanked God: 'Now, Lord, you can let me, your servant, die in peace, as you said'" (Luke 2:28–29).

One look into the face of Jesus, and Simeon knew it was time to go home. And one look into the face of our Savior, and we will know the same.

THREE

THE CRADLE OF HOPE

A Day of Proof and Promise

Christ rose first; then when Christ comes back, all his people will become alive again.

1 CORINTHIANS 15:23 TLB

THE 1989 ARMENIAN EARTHQUAKE NEEDED ONLY FOUR minutes to flatten the nation and kill thirty thousand people. Moments after the deadly tremor ceased, a father raced to an elementary school to save his son. When he arrived, he saw that the building had been leveled. Looking at the mass of stones and rubble, he remembered a promise he had made to his child: "No matter what happens, I'll always be there for you." Driven by his own promise, he found the area closest to his son's room and began to pull back the rocks. Other parents arrived and began sobbing for their children. "It's too late," they told the man. "You know they are dead. You can't help." Even a police officer encouraged him to give up.

But the father refused. For eight hours, then sixteen, then thirty-two, thirty-six hours he dug. His hands were raw and his energy gone, but he refused to quit. Finally, after thirty-eight wrenching hours, he pulled back a boulder and heard his son's voice. He called his boy's name, "Arman! Arman!" And a voice answered him, "Dad, it's me!" Then the boy added these priceless words, "I told the other kids not to worry. I told them if you were alive, you'd save me, and when you saved me, they'd be saved, too. Because you promised, 'No matter what, I'll always be there for you.'"[1]

God has made the same promise to us. "I will come back . . . ," he assures us. Yes, the rocks will tumble. Yes, the ground will shake. But the child of God needn't fear—for the Father has promised to take us to be with him.

But dare we believe the promise? Dare we trust his loyalty? Isn't there a cautious part of us that wonders how reliable these words may be?

Perhaps you have no doubts. If so, you might want to skip this chapter. Others of us, however, could use a reminder. How can we know he will do what he said? How can we believe he will move the rocks and set us free?

Because he's already done it once.

Let's revisit the moment, shall we? Let's sit on the floor, feel the darkness, and be swallowed in the silence as we gaze with the eyes of our hearts where the eyes of our face could never see.

Let's go to the tomb, for Jesus lies in the tomb.

Still. Cold. Stiff. Death has claimed its greatest trophy. He is not asleep in the tomb or resting in the tomb or comatose in the tomb; he is dead in the tomb. No air in his lungs. No thoughts in his brain. No feeling in his limbs. His body is as lifeless as the stone slab upon which he has been laid.

The executioners made sure of it. When Pilate learned that Jesus was dead, he asked the soldiers if they were certain. They were. Had they seen the Nazarene twitch, had they heard even one moan, they would have broken his legs to speed his end. But there was no need. The thrust of a spear removed all doubt. The Romans knew their job. And their job was finished. They pried loose the nails, lowered his body, and gave it to Joseph and Nicodemus.

Joseph of Arimathea. Nicodemus the Pharisee. They sat in seats of power and bore positions of influence. Men of means and men of clout. But they would've traded it all for one breath out of the body of Jesus. He had answered the prayer of their hearts, the prayer for the Messiah. As much as the soldiers wanted him dead, even more these men wanted him alive.

As they sponged the blood from his beard, don't you know they listened for his breath? As they wrapped the cloth around his hands, don't you know they hoped for a pulse? Don't you know they searched for life?

But they didn't find it.

So they do with him what they were expected to do with a dead man. They wrap his body in clean linen and place it in a tomb. Joseph's tomb. Roman guards are stationed to guard the corpse. And a Roman seal is set on the rock of the tomb. For three days, no one gets close to the grave.

But then, Sunday arrives. And with Sunday comes light—a light within the tomb. A bright light? A soft light? Flashing? Hovering? We don't know. But there was a light. For he is the light. And with the light came life. Just as the darkness was banished, now the decay is reversed. Heaven blows and Jesus breathes. His chest expands. Waxy lips open. Wooden fingers lift. Heart valves swish and hinged joints bend.

And, as we envision the moment, we stand in awe.

We stand in awe not just because of what we see, but because of what we know. We know that we, too, will die. We know that we, too, will be buried. Our lungs, like his, will empty. Our hands, like his, will stiffen. But the rising of his body and the rolling of the stone give birth to a mighty belief: "What we believe is this: If we get included in Christ's sin-conquering death, we also get included in his life-saving resurrection. We know that when Jesus was raised from the dead it was a signal of the end of death-as-the-end. Never again will death have the last word. When Jesus died, he took sin down with him, but alive he brings God down to us" (Rom. 6:6–10 MSG).

To the Thessalonians Paul stated: "Since Jesus died and broke loose from the grave, God will most certainly bring back to life those who died in Jesus" (1 Thess. 4:14 MSG).

And to the Corinthians he affirmed: "All who are related to

Christ will rise again. Each, however, in his own turn: Christ rose first; then when Christ comes back, all his people will become alive again" (1 Cor. 15:22–23 TLB).

For Paul and any follower of Christ, the promise is simply this: The resurrection of Jesus is proof and preview of our own.

But can we trust the promise? Is the resurrection a reality? Are the claims of the empty tomb true? This is not only a good question. It is *the* question. For as Paul wrote, "If Christ has not been raised, then your faith has nothing to it; you are still guilty of your sins" (1 Cor. 15:17). In other words, if Christ has been raised, then his followers will join him; but if not, then his followers are fools. The resurrection, then, is the keystone in the arch of the Christian faith. If it be solid, the doorway is trustworthy. Dislodge it and the doorway crumbles.

However, the keystone is not easily budged, for if Jesus is not in the tomb, where is he?

Some speculate he never even died. He was only thought to be dead, but he was actually unconscious. Then he awoke and walked out of the grave. But honestly, how likely is this theory? Jesus endures torturous whippings, thirst and dehydration, nails in his hands and feet, and most of all, a spear in his side. Could a man survive such treatment? And even if he did, could he single-handedly roll back a huge rock from the tomb and then overpower Roman guards and escape? Hardly. Dismiss any thought of Jesus not being dead.

Others accuse the disciples of stealing the body in order to fake the resurrection. They say that Jesus' followers—ordinary tax collectors and fishermen—overcame the sophisticated and well-armed Roman soldiers and detained them long enough to roll back the sealed stone and unwrap the body and escape. Hardly seems plausible, but even if it were, even if the disciples did steal the body, how do we explain their martyrdom? Many of them died for the faith. They died for their belief in the resurrected Lord. Would they fake the resurrection and then die for a hoax? I don't think so. We have to agree with John R. W. Stott, who wrote, "Hypocrites and martyrs are not made of the same stuff."[2]

Some go so far as to claim that the Jews stole the body. Is it possible that Jesus' enemies took the corpse? Perhaps. But why would they? They want the body in the tomb. And we ask just as quickly, if they did steal the body, why didn't they produce it? Display it? Place the carpenter's corpse on a funeral bier and parade it through Jerusalem, and the movement of Jesus would have sizzled like a torch in a lake. But they didn't produce the body. Why? Because they didn't have it.

Christ's death was real. The disciples didn't take his body. The Jews didn't take it. So where is it? Well, during the last two thousand years, millions have opted to accept the simple explanation the angel gave to Mary Magdalene. When she came to visit the grave and found it empty, she was told: "He is not here. He has risen from the dead as he said he would" (Matt. 28:6).

For three days Jesus' body decayed. It did not rest, mind you. It decayed. The cheeks sank and the skin paled. But after three days the process was reversed. There was a stirring, a stirring deep within the grave . . . and the living Christ stepped forth.

And the moment he stepped forth, everything changed. As Paul stated: "When Jesus was raised from the dead it was a signal of the end of death-as-the-end" (Rom. 6:9 MSG).

Don't you love that sentence? "It was a signal of the end of death-as-the-end." The resurrection is an exploding flare announcing to all sincere seekers that it is safe to believe. Safe to believe in ultimate justice. Safe to believe in eternal bodies. Safe to believe in heaven as our estate and the earth as its porch. Safe to believe in a time when questions won't keep us awake and pain won't keep us down. Safe to believe in open graves and endless days and genuine praise.

Because we can accept the resurrection story, it is safe to accept the rest of the story.

Because of the resurrection, everything changes.

Death changes. It used to be the end; now it is the beginning.

The cemetery changes. People once went there to say goodbye; now they go to say, "We'll be together again."

Even the coffin changes. The casket is no longer a box where we hide bodies, but rather a cocoon in which the body is kept until God sets it free to fly.

And someday, according to Christ, he will set us free. He will come back. "I will come back and take you to be with me" (John 14:3). And to prove that he was serious about his promise, the stone was rolled and his body was raised.

For he knows that someday this world will shake again. In the blink of an eye, as fast as the lightning flashes from the east to the west, he will come back. And everyone will see him—you will, I will. Bodies will push back the dirt and break the surface of the sea. The earth will tremble, the sky will roar, and those who do not know him will shudder. But in that hour you will not fear, because you know him.

For you, like the boy in Armenia, have heard the promise of your Father. You know that he has moved the stone—not the stone of the Armenian earthquake, but the stone of the Arimathean's grave. And in the moment he removed the stone, he also removed all reason for doubt. And we, like the boy, can believe the words of our Father: "I will come back and take you to be with me so that you may be where I am" (John 14:3).

Four

Into the Warm Arms of God

A Day of Happy Reunions

He'll come down from heaven and the dead in Christ will rise—
they'll go first. Then the rest of us who are still alive at the time
will be caught up with them into the clouds to meet the Master.
Oh, we'll be walking on air! And then there will be one huge
family reunion with the Master. So reassure one another with
these words.

1 THESSALONIANS 4:16—18 MSG

IF YOU EVER NEED TO BE REMINDED OF THE FRAILTY OF humankind, I have a scene for you to witness. The next time you think people have grown too stoic and self-sufficient, I have a place for you to go. Should you ever worry that hearts are too hard and tears too rare, let me take you to the place where the knees of men buckle and the tears of women flow. Let me take you to a school, and let's watch the parents as they leave their children in class for the very first time.

It's a traumatic event. Long after the school bell has rung and class has begun, adults linger in the parking lot, offering words of comfort and forming support groups. Even though the parents know the school is good, that education is right, and that they'll see their youngster in four short hours, still, they don't want to say good-bye.

We don't like to say good-bye to those we love.

But what is experienced at schools in August is a picnic compared to what is experienced in a cemetery at death. It is one thing to leave loved ones in familiar surroundings. But it is something else entirely to release them into a world we do not know and cannot describe.

We don't like to say good-bye to those we love.

But we have to. Try as we might to avoid it, as reluctant as we are to discuss it, death is a very real part of life. Each one of us must release the hand of one we love into the hand of one we have not seen.

Can you remember the first time death forced you to say good-bye? Most of us can. I can. One day when I was in the third grade, I came home from school surprised to see my father's truck in the driveway. I found him in his bathroom shaving. "Your Uncle Buck died today," he said. His announcement made me feel sad. I liked my uncle. I didn't know him well, but I liked him. The news also made me curious.

At the funeral I heard words like *departed, passed on, gone ahead*. These were unfamiliar terms. I wondered, *Departed to where? Passed on to what? Gone ahead for how long?*

Of course, I've learned since that I'm not the only one with questions about death. Listen in on any discussion about the return of Christ, and someone will inquire, "But what about those who have already died? What happens to Christians between their death and Jesus' return?"

Apparently the church in Thessalonica asked such a question. Listen to Paul's words to them: "We want you to be quite certain, brothers, about those who have died, to make sure that you do not grieve about them, like the other people who have no hope" (1 Thess. 4:13 TJB).

The Thessalonian church had buried her share of loved ones. And Paul wants the members who remain to be at peace regarding the ones who have gone ahead. Many of you have buried loved ones as well. And just as God spoke to them, he speaks to you.

If you'll celebrate a marriage anniversary alone this year, he speaks to you.

If your child made it to heaven before making it to kindergarten, he speaks to you.

If you lost a loved one in violence, if you learned more than you want to know about disease, if your dreams were buried as they lowered the casket, God speaks to you.

He speaks to all of us who have stood or will stand in the soft dirt near an open grave. And to us he gives this confident word: "I want you to know what happens to a Christian when he dies so that when it happens, you will not be full of sorrow, as those are who have no hope. For since we believe that Jesus died and

---

then came back to life again, we can also believe that when Jesus returns, God will bring back with him all the Christians who have died" (1 Thess. 4:13–14 TLB).

God transforms our hopeless grief into hope-filled grief. How? By telling us that we will see our loved ones again.

Bob Russell is a friend of mine who preaches in Kentucky. His father passed away recently. The funeral was held on a cold, blustery, Pennsylvania day. The snow-covered roads precluded the funeral procession, so the director told Bob, "I'll take your dad's body to the grave." Bob couldn't bear the thought of missing his father's burial, so he and his brother and their sons piled into a four-wheel-drive vehicle and followed the hearse. Here is how he described the event:

> We plowed through ten inches of snow into the cemetery, got about fifty yards from my dad's grave, with the wind blowing about twenty-five miles per hour, and the six of us lugged that casket down to the gravesite. . . . We watched the body lowered into the grave and we turned to leave. I felt something was undone, so I said, "I'd like for us to have a prayer." The six of us huddled together and I prayed, "Lord, this is such a cold, lonely place. . . ." And then I got too choked up to pray anymore. I kept battling to get my composure, and finally I just whispered, "But I thank you, for we know to be absent from the body is to be safe in your warm arms."[1]

Isn't that what we want to believe? Just as a parent needs to know that his or her child is safe at school, we long to know that our loved ones are safe in death. We long for the reassurance that the soul goes immediately to be with God. But dare we believe it? Can we believe it? According to the Bible we can.

Scripture is surprisingly quiet about this phase of our lives. When speaking about the period between the death of the body and the resurrection of the body, the Bible doesn't shout; it just whispers. But at the confluence of these whispers, a firm voice is heard. This authoritative voice assures us that, at death, the Christian immediately enters into the presence of God and enjoys conscious fellowship with the Father and with those who have gone before.

Where do I get such ideas? Listen to some of the whispers:

> For to me, to live is Christ and to die is gain. If I am to go on living in the body, this will mean fruitful labor for me. Yet what shall I choose? I do not know! I am torn between the two: I desire to depart and be with Christ, which is better by far. (Phil. 1:21–23 NIV)

The language here suggests an immediate departure of the soul after death. The details of the grammar are a bit tedious but led one scholar to suggest: "What Paul is saying here is that the moment he departs or dies, that very moment he is with the Christ."[2]

Another clue comes from the letter Paul wrote to the Corinthians. Perhaps you've heard the phrase "to be absent from the body is to be at home with the Lord"? Paul used it first: "We really want to be away from the body and be at home with the Lord" (2 Cor. 5:8).

At the second coming of Christ, our bodies will be resurrected. But obviously Paul is not speaking of that in this verse. Otherwise he would not have used the phrase "away from the body." Paul is describing a phase after our death and prior to the resurrection of our bodies. During this time we will be "at home with the Lord."

Isn't this the promise that Jesus gave the thief on the cross? Earlier the thief had rebuked Jesus. Now he repents and asks for mercy. "Remember me when you come into your kingdom" (Luke 23:42). Likely, the thief is praying that he be remembered in some distant time in the future when the kingdom comes. He didn't expect an immediate answer. But he received one: "I tell you the truth, today you will be with me in paradise" (v. 43). The primary message of this passage is God's unlimited and surprising grace. But a secondary message is the immediate translation of the saved into the presence of God. The soul of the believer journeys home, while the body of the believer awaits the resurrection.

As Stephen was being martyred, he saw "heaven open and the Son of Man standing at God's right side" (Acts 7:56). As he was near death he prayed, "Lord Jesus, receive my spirit" (v. 59). It is safe to assume that Jesus did exactly that. Though the body of

Stephen was dead, his spirit was alive. Though his body was buried, his spirit was in the presence of Jesus himself.

Some don't agree with this thought. They propose an intermediate period of purgation, a "holding tank" in which we are punished for our sins. This "purgatory" is the place where, for an undetermined length of time, we receive what our sins deserve so that we can rightly receive what God has prepared.

But two things trouble me about this teaching. For one, none of us can endure what our sins deserve. For another, Jesus already has. The Bible teaches that the wages of sin is death, not purgatory (see Rom. 6:23). The Bible also teaches that Jesus became our purgatory and took our punishment: "When he had brought about the purgation of sins, he took his seat at the right hand of Majesty on high" (Heb. 1:3 NEB). There is no purgatory because purgatory occurred at Calvary.

Others feel that while the body is buried, the soul is asleep. They come by their conviction honestly enough. Seven different times in two different epistles, Paul uses the term *sleep* to refer to death (see 1 Cor. 11:30 NIV; 15:6, 18, 20 NIV; 1 Thess. 4:13–15 NIV). One could certainly deduce that the time spent between death and the return of Christ is spent sleeping. (And, if such is the case, who would complain? We could certainly use the rest!)

But there is one problem. The Bible refers to some who have already died, and they are anything but asleep. Their bodies are sleeping, but their souls are wide awake. Revelation 6:9–11 refers to the souls of martyrs who cry out for justice on the earth.

Matthew 17:3 speaks of Moses and Elijah, who appeared on the Mount of Transfiguration with Jesus. Even Samuel, who came back from the grave, was described wearing a robe and having the appearance of a god (1 Sam. 28:13–14 NASB). And what about the cloud of witnesses who surround us (Heb. 12:1 NASB)? Couldn't these be the heroes of our faith and the loved ones of our lives who have gone before?

I think so. I think Bob's prayer was accurate. When it is cold on earth, we can take comfort in knowing that our loved ones are in the warm arms of God.

We don't like to say good-bye to those whom we love. Whether it be at a school or a cemetery, separation is tough. It is right for us to weep, but there is no need for us to despair. They had pain here. They have no pain there. They struggled here. They have no struggles there. You and I might wonder why God took them home. But they don't. They understand. They are, at this very moment, at peace in the presence of God.

I had been ministering in San Antonio for less than a year when one of our members asked me to speak at the funeral of his mother. Her name was Ida Glossbrenner, but her friends called her Polly.

As the son and I planned the service, he told me a fascinating story about the final words his mother spoke. Mrs. Glossbrenner was unresponsive for the last few hours of her life. She never spoke a word. But moments before her death, she opened her eyes and stated in a clear voice, "My name is Ida Glossbrenner, but my friends call me Polly."

Meaningless words of hallucination? Perhaps. Or, perhaps more. Perhaps Ida was, well, maybe she was at the schoolhouse doors of heaven. Her body behind her. Her soul in the presence of God. And maybe she was getting acquainted.

I don't know. But I do know this. When it is cold on earth, we can take comfort in knowing that our loved ones are in the warm arms of God. And when Christ comes, we will hold them, too.

FIVE

THE BRAND-NEW YOU

A Day of Rejuvenation

> *There is an order to this resurrection: Christ was raised first; then*
> *when Christ comes back, all his people will be raised.*

1 CORINTHIANS 15:23 NLT

SUPPOSE YOU WERE WALKING PAST MY FARM ONE DAY and saw me in the field crying. (I don't have a farm nor am I prone to sitting in fields, but play along with me.) There I sit, disconsolate at the head of a furrowed row. Concerned, you approach me and ask what is wrong. I look up from beneath my John Deere tractor hat and extend a palm full of seeds in your direction. "My heart breaks for the seeds," I weep. "My heart breaks for the seeds."

"What?"

Between sobs I explain, "The seeds will be placed in the ground and covered with dirt. They will decay, and we will never see them again."

As I weep, you are stunned. You look around for a turnip truck off which you are confident I tumbled. Finally, you explain to me a basic principle of farming: out of the decay of the seed comes the birth of a plant.

You put a finger in my face and kindly remind me: "Do not bemoan the burial of the seed. Don't you know that you will soon witness a mighty miracle of God? Given time and tender care, this tiny kernel will break from its prison of soil and blossom into a plant far beyond its dreams."

Well, maybe you aren't that dramatic, but those are your thoughts. Any farmer who grieves over the burial of a seed needs a reminder: a time of planting is not a time of grief. Any person who anguishes over the burial of a body may need the same. We may need the reminder Paul gave the Corinthians. "There is an order to this resurrection: Christ was raised first; then when Christ comes back, all his people will be raised" (1 Cor. 15:23 NLT).

In the last chapter we looked at what happens to the Christian between the death of the body and the return of our Savior. In this phase, Scripture assures us that our souls are living, but our body is buried. This is an intermediate period in which we are "away from this body and . . . at home with the Lord" (2 Cor. 5:8).

Upon death, our souls will journey immediately to the presence of God while we await the resurrection of our bodies. And when will this resurrection occur? You guessed it. When Christ comes. "When Christ comes again, those who belong to him will be raised to life, and then the end will come" (1 Cor. 15:23–24).

This kind of verse stirs a classroom of questions: What does

Paul mean, "those who belong to him will be raised to life"? What will be raised? My body? If so, why *this* body? I don't like my body. Why don't we start over on a new model?

Come with me back to the farm, and let's look for some answers.

If you were impressed with my seed allegory, I'd better be honest. I stole the idea from the apostle Paul. The fifteenth chapter of his letter to the Corinthians is the definitive essay on our resurrection. We won't study the entire chapter, but we will isolate a few verses and make a few points.

He writes: "But someone may ask, 'How are the dead raised? What kind of body will they have?' Foolish person! When you sow a seed, it must die in the ground before it can live and grow. And when you sow it, it does not have the same 'body' it will have later. What you sow is only a bare seed, maybe wheat or something else. But God gives it a body that he has planned for it" (1 Cor. 15:35–38).

In other words: You can't have a new body without the death of the old body.[1] Or, as Paul says, "When you sow a seed, it must die in the ground before it can live and grow" (v. 36).

A friend told me that Paul's parallel between seeds sown and bodies buried reminded her of a remark made by her youngest son. He was a first grader, and his class was studying plants about the same time the family attended a funeral of a loved one. One day, as they were driving past a cemetery, the two events came together in one statement. "Hey, Mom," he volunteered, pointing toward the graveyard. "That's where they plant people."

The apostle Paul would have liked that. In fact, Paul would like us to change the way we think about the burial process. The graveside service is not a burial, but a planting. The grave is not a hole in the ground, but a fertile furrow. The cemetery is not the resting place, but rather the transformation place.

Most assume that death has no purpose. It is to people what the black hole is to space—a mysterious, inexplicable, distasteful, all-consuming power. Avoid it at all costs. And so we do! We do all we can to live and not die. God, however, says we must die in order to live. When you sow a seed, it must die in the ground before it can grow (v. 36). What we see as the ultimate tragedy, he sees as the ultimate triumph.

And when a Christian dies, it's not a time to despair, but a time to trust. Just as the seed is buried and the material wrapping decomposes, so our fleshly body will be buried and will decompose. But just as the buried seed sprouts new life, so our body will blossom into a new body. As Jesus said, "Unless a grain of wheat falls into the earth and dies, it remains a single grain of wheat; but if it dies, it brings a good harvest" (John 12:24 PHILLIPS).

If you'll permit a sudden shift of metaphors, let me jump from plants and a farm to dinner and dessert. Don't we love to be enticed by dessert? Don't we love to hear the cook say, "As soon as you are finished, I have a surprise for you"? God says something similar regarding our body. "Let's finish with the one you have, and then I have a surprise."

What is this surprise? What is this new body I will receive?

Again, our seed analogy helps. Paul wrote, "When you sow it [the seed], it does not have the same 'body' it will have later" (1 Cor. 15:37). Meaning, we can't envision the new body by looking at the old body.

I think you'll appreciate the way Eugene Peterson paraphrases this text:

> There are no diagrams for this kind of thing. We do have a parallel experience in gardening. You plant a "dead" seed; soon there is a flourishing plant. There is no visual likeness between seed and plant. You could never guess what a tomato would look like by looking at a tomato seed. What we plant in the soil and what grows out of it don't look anything alike. The dead body that we bury in the ground and the resurrection body that comes from it will be dramatically different. (1 Cor. 15:36–38 MSG)

Paul's point is clear. You can't envision the glory of the plant by staring at the seed, nor can you garner a glimpse of your future body by studying the present one. All we know is that this body will be changed.

"Come on, Paul, just give us a clue. Just a hint. Can't you tell us a little more about our new bodies?"

Apparently he knew we would ask, for the apostle stays on the subject for a few more paragraphs and provides one final point. You may not be able to envision it, but one thing's for sure: you are going to love your new body.

Paul outlines three ways God will transform our bodies. Our bodies will be changed from:

1. Corruption to incorruption—"The body is sown in corruption, it is raised in incorruption" (v. 42 NKJV).
2. Dishonor to glory—"It is sown in dishonor, it is raised in glory" (v. 43 NKJV).
3. Weakness to power—"It is sown in weakness, it is raised in power" (v. 43 NKJV).

Corruption. Dishonor. Weakness. Three unflattering words used to describe our bodies. But who would argue with them?

Julius Schniewind didn't. He was a highly regarded European Bible scholar. In the final weeks of his life, he battled a painful kidney disease. His biographer tells how, one night, after the professor had led a Bible study, he was putting on his coat to go home. As he did, the severe pain in his side caused him to groan aloud the Greek phrase *"Soma tapeinõseõs, soma tapeinõseõs."* The student of Scripture was quoting the words of Paul, "For our citizenship is in heaven, from which we also eagerly wait for the Savior, the Lord Jesus Christ, who will transform our lowly body [*soma tapeinõseõs*]" (Phil. 3:20–21 NKJV).[2]

You and I don't go about mumbling Greek phrases, but we do know what it is like to live in a lowly body. In fact, some of you know all too well. Out of curiosity I made a list of the news I've heard in the last twenty-four hours concerning failing health. Here is what has come my way:

- A professor was diagnosed with Parkinson's disease.
- A middle-aged man is concerned about his test results. We learn tomorrow if he has cancer.
- A friend's father is scheduled for eye surgery.
- Another friend had a stroke.
- A minister died after four decades of preaching.

Can you relate? You probably can. In fact, I wonder if God wants to use the next few lines to speak directly to you. Your body is so tired, so worn. Joints ache and muscles fatigue. You understand why Paul described the body as a tent. "We groan in this tent," he wrote (2 Cor. 5:2). Your tent used to be sturdy and strong, but the seasons have passed and the storms have raged, and this old canvas has some bare spots. Chilled by the cold, bowed by the wind, your tent is not as strong as it used to be.

Or, then again, maybe your "tent," your body, never has been strong. Your sight never has been crisp; your hearing never has been clear. Your walk never has been sturdy; your heart never has been steady. You've watched others take for granted the health you've never had. Wheelchairs, doctor visits, hospital rooms, needles, stethoscopes—if you never saw another one for the rest of your life, you'd be happy. You'd give anything, yes, anything, for one full day in a strong, healthy body.

If that describes you, let God speak to your heart for just a moment. The purpose of this book is to use the return of Christ to encourage the heart. Few people need encouragement more than the physically afflicted. And few verses encourage more than

Philippians 3:20–21. We read verse 20 a few paragraphs ago; you'll relish verse 21: "He will take these dying bodies of ours and change them into glorious bodies like his own" (TLB).

Let's sample a couple of other versions of this verse:

"He will transfigure these wretched bodies of ours into copies of his glorious body" (TJB).

"He will transfigure the body belonging to our humble state, and give it a form like that of his own resplendent body" (NEB).

Regardless of the wording, the promise is the same. Your body will be changed. You will not receive a different body; you will receive a renewed body. Just as God can make an oak out of a kernel or a tulip out of a bulb, he makes a "new" body out of the old one. A body without corruption. A body without weakness. A body without dishonor. A body identical to the body of Jesus.

My friend Joni Eareckson Tada makes this same point. Rendered a quadriplegic by a teenage diving accident, the last two decades have been spent in discomfort. She, more than most, knows the meaning of living in a lowly body. At the same time, she more than most, knows the hope of a resurrected body. Listen to her words:

> Somewhere in my broken, paralyzed body is the seed of what I
> shall become. The paralysis makes what I am to become all the
> more grand when you contrast atrophied, useless legs against
> splendorous resurrected legs. I'm convinced that if there are
> mirrors in heaven (and why not?), the image I'll see will be

unmistakably "Joni," although a much better, brighter Joni. So much so, that it's not worth comparing. . . . I will bear the likeness of Jesus, the man from heaven.[3]

Would you like a sneak preview of your new body? We have one by looking at the resurrected body of our Lord. After his resurrection, Jesus spent forty days in the presence of people. The resurrected Christ was not in a disembodied, purely spiritual state. On the contrary, he had a body—a touchable, visible body.

Just ask Thomas. Thomas said he wouldn't believe in the resurrection unless "I . . . put my finger where the nails were and put my hand into his side" (John 20:25). The response of Christ? He appeared to Thomas and said, "Put your finger here, and look at my hands. Put your hand here in my side. Stop being an unbeliever and believe" (v. 27).

Jesus didn't come as a mist or a wind or a ghostly specter. He came in a body. A body that maintained a substantial connection with the body he originally had. A body that had flesh and bones. For did he not tell his followers, "A spirit has not flesh and bones as you see that I have" (Luke 24:39 RSV)?

Jesus' resurrected body, then, was a real body, real enough to walk on the road to Emmaus, real enough to appear in the form of a gardener, real enough to eat breakfast with the disciples at Galilee. Jesus had a real body.[4]

At the same time, this body was not a clone of his earthly body. Mark tells us that Jesus "appeared in another form" (Mark

16:12 RSV). While he was the same, he was different. So different that Mary Magdalene, his disciples on the sea, and his disciples on the path to Emmaus did not recognize him. Though he invited Thomas to touch his body, he passed through a closed door to be in Thomas's presence.[5]

So what do we know about the resurrected body of Jesus? It was unlike any the world had ever seen.

What do we know about our resurrected bodies? They will be unlike any we have ever imagined.

Will we look so different that we aren't instantly recognized? Perhaps. (We may need nametags.) Will we be walking through walls? Chances are we'll be doing much more.

Will we still bear the scars from the pain of life? The marks of war. The disfigurements of disease. The wounds of violence. Will these remain on our bodies? That is a very good question. Jesus, at least for forty days, kept his. Will we keep ours? On this issue, we have only opinions, but my opinion is that we won't. Peter tells us that "by his wounds you have been healed" (1 Peter 2:24 NIV). In heaven's accounting, only one wound is worthy to be remembered. And that is the wound of Jesus. Our wounds will be no more.

God is going to renew your body and make it like his. What difference should this make in the way you live?

Your body, in some form, will last forever. Respect it.

You will live forever in this body. It will be different, mind you. What is now crooked will be straightened. What is now faulty will be fixed. Your body will be different, but you won't have a different body. You will have this one. Does that change the view you have of it? I hope so.

God has a high regard for your body. You should as well. Respect it. I did not say worship it. But I did say respect it. It is, after all, the temple of God (see 1 Cor. 6:19). Be careful how you feed it, use it, and maintain it. You wouldn't want anyone trashing your home; God doesn't want anyone trashing his. After all, it is his, isn't it? A little jogging and dieting to the glory of God wouldn't hurt most of us. Your body, in some form, will last forever. Respect it.

I have one final thought.

Your pain will NOT last forever. Believe it.

Are your joints arthritic? They won't be in heaven.

Is your heart weak? It will be strong in heaven.

Has cancer corrupted your system? There is no cancer in heaven.

Are your thoughts disjointed? Your memory failing? Your new body will have a new mind.

Does this body seem closer to death than ever before? It should. It is. And unless Christ comes first, your body will be buried. Like a seed is placed in the ground, so your body will be placed in a tomb. And for a season, your soul will be in heaven while your body is in the grave. But the seed buried in the earth will blossom in heaven. Your soul and body will reunite, and you will be like Jesus.

Six

A New Wardrobe

A Day of Redemption

Live in him so that when Christ comes back, we can be without
fear and not be ashamed in his presence.

1 JOHN 2:28

I MAKE NO CLAIMS TO BEING A GOOD GOLFER, BUT I READILY
confess to being a golf addict. If you know of a twelve-step program
for the condition, sign me up. "Hi, I'm Max. I'm a golfaholic." I love
to play golf, watch golf, and, on good nights, I even dream golf.

Knowing this will help you appreciate the extreme joy I felt
when I was invited to attend the Masters Golf Tournament. A pass
to the Masters is the golfer's Holy Grail. Tickets are as scarce as
birdies on my scorecard. So, I was thrilled. The invitation came
via pro golfer Scott Simpson. Each player is given a certain number of passes, and Scott offered Denalyn and me two of his. (If
there was ever any question about Scott's place in heaven, that
gesture erased the doubt.)

So off we went to Augusta National Country Club in Augusta, Georgia, where golf heritage hangs like moss from the trees. There you find the green where Nicklaus sank *the* putt. The fringe where Mize holed *the* chip. The fairway where Sarazen hit *the* approach shot. I was a kid in a candy store. And, like a kid, I couldn't get enough. It wasn't enough to see the course and walk the grounds, I wanted to see the locker room. That's where the clubs of Hogan and Azinger are displayed. That's where the players hang out. And that's where I wanted to be.

But they wouldn't let me. A guard stopped me at the entrance. I showed him my pass, but he shook his head. I told him I knew Scott, but that didn't matter. I promised to send his eldest child through college, but he didn't budge. "Only caddies and players," he explained. Well, he knew I wasn't a player. He also knew I wasn't a caddie. Caddies at the Masters are required to wear white coveralls. My clothing was a dead giveaway. So I left, figuring I'd never see the clubhouse. I had made it all the way to the door but was denied entrance.

Many, many people fear the same will happen to them. Not at Augusta, but in heaven. They fear being turned away at the door. A legitimate fear, don't you think? We're talking about a pivotal moment. To be turned away from seeing golf history is one thing, but to be refused admission into heaven is quite another.

That is why some people don't want to discuss the return of Christ. It makes them nervous. They may be God-fearing and church-attending but still nervous. Is there a solution for this fear? Need you spend the rest of your life wondering if you will be turned away at the door? Yes, there is a solution and, no, you don't have to worry. According to the Bible, it is possible to "know beyond the shadow of a doubt that you have eternal life" (1 John 5:13 MSG). How? How can any of us know for sure?

Curiously, it all has to do with the clothing we wear.

Jesus explained the matter in one of his parables. He tells the story of a king who plans a wedding party for his son. Invitations are given, but the people "refused to come" (Matt. 22:3). The king is patient and offers another invitation. This time the servants of the king are mistreated and killed. The king is furious. The murderers are punished and the city is destroyed and the invitation is re-extended, this time, to everyone.

The application of the parable is not complicated. God invited Israel, his chosen ones, to be his children. But they refused. Not only did they refuse, they killed his servants and crucified his son. The consequence was the judgment of God. Jerusalem was burned and the people were scattered.

As the parable continues, the king offers yet another invitation. This time the wedding was opened to everyone—"good and bad," or Jews and Gentiles. Here is where we non-Jews appear in the parable. We are the beneficiaries of a wide invitation. And someday, when Christ comes, we will stand at the entryway to the king's castle. But the story doesn't end there. Standing at the doorway is not enough. A certain wardrobe is required. The parable ends with a chilling paragraph.

Let's pick up the story at the end of verse 10:

And the wedding hall was filled with guests. When the king came in to see the guests, he saw a man who was not dressed for a wedding. The king said, "Friend, how were you allowed to come in here? You are not dressed for a wedding." But the man said nothing. So the king told some servants, "Tie this man's hands and feet. Throw him out into the darkness, where people will cry and grind their teeth with pain." (Matt. 22:10–13)

Jesus loved surprise endings, and this one surprises . . . and frightens. Here is a man who was at the right place, surrounded by the right people, but dressed in the wrong garment. And because he wore the wrong clothing, he was cast from the presence of the king.

"Wrong clothes? Max, are you telling me that Jesus cares what clothes we wear?"

Apparently so. In fact, the Bible tells us exactly the wardrobe God desires.

"But clothe yourselves with the Lord Jesus Christ and forget about satisfying your sinful self" (Rom. 13:14).

"You were all baptized into Christ, and so you were all clothed with Christ. This means that you are all children of God through faith in Christ Jesus" (Gal. 3:26–27).

This clothing has nothing to do with dresses and jeans and suits. God's concern is with our spiritual garment. He offers a heavenly robe that only heaven can see and only heaven can give. Listen to the words of Isaiah: "The LORD makes me very happy; all that I am rejoices in my God. He has covered me with clothes of salvation and wrapped me with a coat of goodness" (Isa. 61:10).

Remember the words of the father when the prodigal son returned? He wanted his son to have new sandals, a new ring, and what else? New clothes. "Bring the best clothes and put them on him" (Luke 15:22). No son of his was going to be seen in shabby, muddy rags. The father wanted the son to have the best clothing available.

Your Father wants you to have the same.

Again, this discussion of clothing has nothing to do with what the store sells you. It has everything to do with what God gives you when you give your life to him. Let me explain.

When a person becomes a follower of Christ, when sins are confessed and the grace of Jesus is accepted, a wonderful miracle of the soul occurs. The person is placed "in" Christ. The apostle Paul described himself as "a man in Christ" (2 Cor. 12:2). When he described his colleagues, he called them "fellow workers in Christ Jesus" (Rom 16:3 NIV). The greatest promise is extended, not to the wealthy or educated, but to those who are "in Christ." "Therefore, there is now no condemnation for those who are *in Christ Jesus*" (Rom. 8:1 NIV, emphasis mine). John urges us to "live in him so that when Christ comes back, we can be without fear and not ashamed in his presence" (1 John 2:28).

What does it mean to be "in Christ"? The clothing illustration is a good one. Why do we wear clothes? There are parts of our body we want to hide.

The same can be true with our spiritual lives. Do we want God to see everything about us? No. If he did, we would be fearful and ashamed. How could we ever hope to go to heaven with all our mistakes showing? "The true life," Paul says, "is a hidden one in God, through Christ" (Col. 3:3 PHILLIPS).

Let's take this a step further. Let's imagine how a person who isn't wearing the clothing of Christ appears in the eyes of heaven. For the sake of discussion, envision a decent human being . . . we'll call him Danny Decent. Danny, from our perspective, does everything right. He pays his taxes, pays his bills, pays attention to his family, and pays respect to his superiors. He is a good person. In fact, were we to dress him, we would dress him in white.

But heaven sees Danny differently. God sees what you and I miss. For as Mr. Decent walks through life, he makes mistakes. And every time he sins, a stain appears on his clothing. For example, he stretched the truth when he spoke to his boss yesterday. He was stained. He fudged, ever so slightly, on his expense report. Another stain. The other guys were gossiping about the new employee and, rather than walk away, he chimed in. Still another. From our perspective, these aren't big deals. But our perspective doesn't matter. God's does. And what God sees is a man wrapped in mistakes.

Unless something happens, Danny will be the man in the parable, the one without the wedding garment. The wedding garment, you see, is the righteousness of Christ. And if Danny faces Christ wearing his own decency instead of Christ's goodness, he will hear what the man in the parable heard. "'You are not dressed for a wedding.' . . . So the king told some servants, 'Tie this man's hands and feet. Throw him out into the darkness, where people will cry and grind their teeth with pain'" (Matt. 22:12–13).

What happens if Danny changes his clothes? What if he agrees with Isaiah, who said, "Our righteous acts are like filthy rags" (Isa. 64:6 NIV)? Suppose he goes to Christ and prays, "Lord, take away these rags. Clothe me in your grace." Suppose he confesses the prayer of this hymn: "Weary, come to Thee for rest, naked come to Thee for dress."[1]

If he does, here is what happens. Jesus, in an act visible only to the eyes of heaven, removes the robe of stains and replaces it with his robe of righteousness. As a result, Danny is clothed in Christ. And, as a result, Danny is dressed for the wedding.

To quote another hymn: "Dressed in His righteousness alone, faultless to stand before the throne."[2]

God has only one requirement for entrance into heaven: that we be clothed in Christ.

Listen to how Jesus describes the inhabitants of heaven: "They will walk with me and wear white clothes, because they are worthy. Those who win the victory will be dressed in white clothes like them. And I will not erase their names from the book of life, but I will say they belong to me before my Father and before his angels" (Rev. 3:4–5).

Listen to the description of the elders: "Around the throne there were twenty-four other thrones with twenty-four elders sitting on them. They were dressed in white and had golden crowns on their heads" (Rev. 4:4).

And what is the clothing of the angels? "The armies of heaven, dressed in fine linen, white and clean, were following him on white horses" (Rev. 19:14).

All are dressed in white. The saints. The elders. The armies. How would you suppose Jesus is dressed? In white?

You'd think so. Of all the people worthy to wear a spotless robe, Christ is. But according to the Bible he doesn't. "Then I saw heaven opened, and there before me was a white horse. The rider on the horse is called Faithful and True, and he is right when he judges and makes war. His eyes are like burning fire, and on his head are many crowns. He has a name written on him, which no one but himself knows. He is dressed in a robe dipped in blood, and his name is the Word of God" (Rev. 19:11–13).

Why is Christ's robe not white? Why is his cloak not spotless? Why is his garment dipped in blood? Let me answer by reminding you what Jesus did for you and me. Paul says simply, "He changed places with us" (Gal. 3:13).

He did more than remove our coat; he put on our coat. And he wore our coat of sin to the cross. As he died, his blood flowed over our sins. They were cleansed by his blood. And because of this, when Christ comes, we have no fear of being turned away at the door.

Speaking of being turned away at the door, did I fail to tell you the rest of the Masters Golf Tournament story? I'm sure you are dying to hear whether or not I made it into the locker room. Well, wouldn't you know it, I did.

The day prior to the tournament, the golfers play an exhibition round on a par-three course. It is customary for the golfers to give their caddie the afternoon off and invite a friend or family member to take his place. Well, Scott invited me to be his caddie. "Of course, you'll have to wear the white overalls," he explained.

And, of course, I didn't mind. *Snicker.*

That afternoon, when the round was over, I made my way to the clubhouse. And through the same door, walking past the same guard, I stepped into golf's inner sanctum. What made the difference? One day I was turned away, the next I was welcomed. Why the change?

Simple, I was wearing the right clothes.

SEVEN

LOOK WHO'S IN THE WINNER'S CIRCLE!

A Day of Rewards

> *When the master comes and finds the servant doing his work, the servant will be blessed.*
>
> MATTHEW 24:46

IT'S SUNDAY, SEPTEMBER 27, 1998. EVEN THOUGH THE St. Louis Cardinals have no hope of making the Major League Baseball playoffs, the ballpark is packed. It was packed three weeks earlier when Mark McGwire tied Roger Maris's home run record with a 430-foot shot off the stadium club window. It was packed the next day when 46,100 fans, as well as half of the human race, watched him break the record with a clothesline shot over the left field fence.

And it is packed today. Since Friday, McGwire has hit not one or two home runs, but three. For thirty-seven years, no one could hit more than sixty-one homers in one season; now the St. Louis slugger has hit sixty-eight. And he isn't finished. Number sixty-nine lands in the left field seats. It takes two curtain calls to silence the crowd. Home run number seventy comes in the seventh inning. The fans are on their feet before he comes to bat; they stay on their feet long after he crosses the plate.

They cheer the home run. They cheer the new record. They cheer the fellow who caught the ball. They cheer the season. And they cheer something else.

I'm speculating now. But I really believe that they—and we— cheered something else. We cheered because he did what we wanted to do. Wasn't there a time when you wanted to be where Mark McGwire was? Think a little. Scroll back a bit. Wasn't there a younger, more idealistic you who dreamed of hitting the big ball? Or winning the Pulitzer? Or singing on Broadway? Or commanding a fleet? Or receiving the Nobel Peace Prize? Or clutching an Oscar?

Wasn't there a time when you stepped up to the plate with a bat on your shoulder and stars in your eyes? Just a few years and Little League would become the big leagues and watch out Babe, watch out Mickey, watch out Roger—here I come!

But most of us don't make it. Bats are traded for calculators or stethoscopes or computers. And, with only slight regret, we set about the task of making a living. We understand. Not everyone can be a Mark McGwire. For every million who aspire, only one achieves. The vast majority of us don't hit the big ball, don't feel the ticker tape, don't wear the gold medal, don't give the valedictory address.

———

And that's OK. We understand that in the economy of earth, there are a limited number of crowns.

The economy of heaven, however, is refreshingly different. Heavenly rewards are not limited to a chosen few, but "to all those who have waited with love for him to come again" (2 Tim. 4:8). The three-letter word *all* is a gem. The winner's circle isn't reserved for a handful of the elite, but for a heaven full of God's children who "will receive the crown of life that God has promised to those who love him" (James 1:12 NIV).

From the mouth of Jesus, we hear a similar promise: The saved of Christ will receive their reward. "When the master comes and finds the servant doing his work, the servant will be blessed" (Matt. 24:46).

The promise is echoed in the Epistles: "The Lord will reward everyone for whatever good he does, whether he is slave or free" (Eph. 6:8 NIV).

And in the Beatitudes: "Rejoice and be glad, because great is your reward in heaven" (Matt. 5:12 NIV).

For all we don't know about the next life, this much is certain. The day Christ comes will be a day of reward. Those who went unknown on earth will be known in heaven. Those who never heard the cheers of men will hear the cheers of angels. Those who missed the blessing of a father will hear the blessing of their heavenly Father. The small will be great. The forgotten will be remembered. The unnoticed will be crowned and the faithful will be honored. What McGwire heard in the shadow of the St. Louis Arch will be nothing compared to what you will hear in the presence of God. McGwire received a Corvette. You'll receive a crown—not just one crown, but three. Would you enjoy a preview?

The crown of life. "Blessed is the man who perseveres under trial, because when he has stood the test, he will receive the crown of life that God has promised to those who love him" (James 1:12 NIV).

To help you appreciate eternity, consider this rule of thumb: Heaven will be wonderful, not only because of what is present, but because of what is absent. Say that again? I'll be glad to. *Heaven will be wonderful, not only because of what is present, but because of what is absent.*

As the apostle John took notes on what he saw in heaven, he was careful to mention what was absent. Remember his famous list of "no mores"? God "will wipe away every tear from their eyes, and there will be no more death, sadness, crying, or pain, because all the old ways are gone" (Rev. 21:4).

Did you catch the first "no more"? *There will be no more death.* Can you imagine a world with no death, only life? If you can, you can imagine heaven. For citizens of heaven wear the crown of life.

What have you done today to avoid death? Likely a lot. You've popped pills, pumped pecs, passed on the pie, and pursued the polyunsaturates. (Please pardon the perpetuity of p's in this paragraph.) Why? Why the effort? Because you are worried about staying alive. That won't be a worry in heaven.

In fact, you won't be worrying at all. Some of you moms

worry about your kids getting hurt. You won't worry in heaven. In heaven we'll feel no pain. Some of you fellows worry about getting old. You won't in heaven. We'll all be ceaselessly strong. You travelers worry about the plane crashing. You won't in heaven. Heaven has no planes that I know of. If it does, they don't crash. But if they crash, no one dies. So you don't have to worry.

Last summer I hurt my back. The injury was nothing serious, but enough to wake me up. I needed to get in better shape. So I set out on an exercise regimen that was, if I say so myself, pretty strict. In time the back muscles were strengthened, my weight was down, and I was feeling pretty strong. I was beginning to field calls from professional football teams, weightlifting magazines, and modeling agencies, when I came very close to losing it all. A lady ran a red light and nearly hit me. We avoided the collision and kept going, but it was close. My sculpted physique could have been hurt! As I was driving away, this goofy thought popped in my head: *Is that my reward for all my exercise? I mean, I run, eat right, lift weights, and, through no fault of my own, it could be gone in a second.*

Isn't that the way life goes? We are frail creatures. Of course, my experience is small compared to the loss of others. Consider the mother who gives birth only to be rewarded with a stillborn child. Consider the man who works hard to retire, only to have retirement cut short by cancer. Consider the high school athlete who trains hard, only to be injured. We are not made of steel, we are made of dust. And this life is not crowned with life, it is crowned with death.

The next life, however, is different. Jesus urged the Christians in Smyrna to "be faithful, even if you have to die, and I will give you the crown of life" (Rev. 2:10).

Let me suggest another crown we'll receive in heaven.

The crown of righteousness. "I have done my best in the race, I have run the full distance, and I have kept the faith. And now there is waiting for me the victory prize of being put right with God, which the Lord, the righteous Judge, will give me on that Day—and not only to me, but to all those who wait with love for him to appear" (2 Tim. 4:7–8 TEV).

The word *righteousness* defines itself. It means, simply, to be in a right relationship with God. The apostle Paul looks toward the day when he is crowned in righteousness. Now, the careful Bible student might raise a question here. Aren't we already righteous? Didn't I just read a chapter that stated that we are clothed in righteousness when we become Christians? Yes, you did.

Then why do we also receive a crown of righteousness? What happens in heaven that hasn't happened on earth? That is a good question and can be answered by using a favorite analogy of the apostle Paul, the analogy of adoption.

While we lived in Rio de Janeiro, we met several American families who came to Brazil to adopt children. They would spend days, sometimes weeks, immersed in a different language and a strange culture. They fought the red tape and paid the large fees, all with the hope of taking a child to the United States.

In some cases the adoption was completed before the child was born. For financial reasons, the couple would often have to return to the U.S. while awaiting the birth of their child. Think about their position: The papers have been signed, the money has been given, but the child is not yet born. They must wait until the birth before they can return to Brazil and claim the child.

Hasn't God done the same for us? He entered our culture, battled the resistance, and paid the unspeakable price which adoption required. Legally we are his. He owns us. We have every legal privilege accorded to a child. We are just waiting for him to return. We are, as Paul said, "waiting for God to finish making us his own children" (Rom. 8:23).

We are in a right relationship now; we are clothed with Christ. But when Jesus comes, the relationship will be made even "righter." (I know that's not a word.) Our wardrobe will be complete. We will be crowned with righteousness. We will be rightly related to God.

Think about what that means. What prevents people from being rightly related to God? Sin. And if heaven promises a right relationship with God, what is missing in heaven? You got it, baby. Sin. Heaven will be sin-free. Both death and sin will be things of the past.

Is this a big deal? I think so. Earlier we tried to imagine a world with no death; let's do the same with sin. Can you imagine a world minus sin? Have you done anything recently because of sin?

At the very least, you've complained. You've worried. You've grumbled. You've hoarded when you should have shared. You've

---

turned away when you should have helped. You've second-guessed, and you've covered up. But you won't do that in heaven.

Because of sin, you've snapped at the ones you love and argued with the ones you cherish. You have felt ashamed, guilty, bitter. You have ulcers, sleepless nights, cloudy days, and a pain in the neck. But you won't have those in heaven.

Because of sin, the young are abused and the elderly forgotten. Because of sin, God is cursed and drugs are worshiped. Because of sin, the poor have less and the affluent want more. Because of sin, babies have no daddies and husbands have no wives. But in heaven, sin will have no power; in fact, sin will have no presence. There will be no sin.

Sin has sired a thousand heartaches and broken a million promises. Your addiction can be traced back to sin. Your mistrust can be traced back to sin. Bigotry, robbery, adultery—all because of sin. But in heaven, all of this will end.

Can you imagine a world without sin? If so, you can imagine heaven.

Let me make this promise more practical. Some time ago a friend asked a very honest question about eternity. It had to do with his ex-wife. She is now a Christian and he is now a Christian. But things are still icy between them. He wondered how he would feel when he saw her in heaven.

I told him he would feel great. I told him he would be thrilled to see her. Why? Well, what causes tension between people? In a word, *sin*. If there is no sin, there is no tension. None. No tension between ex and ex, between black and white, between abused and abuser, even between the murdered and the repentant murderer.

The beautiful prophecy of Isaiah 11 will come true: "Then wolves will live in peace with lambs, and leopards will lie down to rest with goats. Calves, lions, and young bulls will eat together, and a little child will lead them" (Isa. 11:6).

Almost a millennium later John made a similar promise. Heaven will be great, he said, not just because of what is present, but because of what is missing. God "will wipe away every tear from their eyes, and there will be no more death, sadness, crying, or pain, because all the old ways are gone" (Rev. 21:4).

John's list could have gone on forever. Since heaven has no sin or death there will be no more _____. You fill in the blank. No more aspirin. Chemotherapy. Wheelchairs. Divorce. Jail cells or broken hearts. Crippled limbs or car wrecks.

To be crowned in life means no more death. To be crowned in righteousness means no more sin. And to be crowned in glory means no more defeat.

Let's look at this last crown.

The crown of glory. "And when the Chief Shepherd appears, you will receive the crown of glory that will never fade away" (1 Peter 5:4 NIV).

It's worthy of note that Mark McGwire almost gave up. He almost quit baseball in high school so he could play golf. But he didn't. Something pulled him back. A few years into his career, he almost quit again. Neither his marriage nor the season was anything to write home about. He told his wife he was going to quit, but something made him return. Then there were the foot injuries. From '92 to '95 he endured multiple surgeries and missed two-thirds of the games. He told his parents he was going to quit. But something made him stay.

What made him stay? A dream. Somewhere he got the idea that he could do it. Long before his name was mentioned in the same breath with Ruth and Maris, long before he was called the St. Louis slugger or Big Mac, long before the fans thought he could, he thought he could. He dreamed of beating the record. He set his eyes on the prize, and he didn't give up.

May I close with a special word to a special group? Some of you have never won a prize in your life. Oh, maybe you were quartermaster in your Boy Scout troop or in charge of sodas at the homeroom Christmas party, but that's about it. You've never won much. You've watched the Mark McGwires of this world carry home the trophies and walk away with the ribbons. All you have are "almosts" and "what ifs."

If that hits home, then you'll cherish this promise: "And when the Chief Shepherd appears, you will receive the crown of glory that will never fade away" (1 Peter 5:4 NIV).

Your day is coming. What the world has overlooked, your Father has remembered, and sooner than you can imagine, you will be blessed by him. Look at this promise from the pen of Paul: "God will praise each one of them" (1 Cor. 4:5).

What an incredible sentence. *God will praise each one of them.*

Not "the best of them" nor "a few of them" nor "the achievers among them," but "God will praise each one of them."

You won't be left out. God will see to that. In fact, God himself will give the praise. When it comes to giving recognition, God does not delegate the job. Michael doesn't hand out the crowns. Gabriel doesn't speak on behalf of the throne. God himself does the honors. God himself will praise his children.

And what's more, the praise is personal! Paul says, "God will praise each one of them" (1 Cor. 4:5). Awards aren't given a nation at a time, a church at a time, or a generation at a time. The crowns are given one at a time. God himself will look you in the eye and bless you with the words, "Well done, good and faithful servant! You have been faithful with a few things; I will put you in charge of many things. Come and share your master's happiness!" (Matt. 25:23 NIV).

With that in mind, let me urge you to stay strong. Don't give up. Don't look back. Let Jesus speak to your heart as he says, "Hold on to what you have, so that no one will take your crown" (Rev. 3:11 NIV).

Eight

You'd Do It All Again

A Day of Sweet Surprises

You are our hope, our joy, and the crown we will take pride in when our Lord Jesus Christ comes.

1 THESSALONIANS 2:19

OSKAR SCHINDLER HAD HIS SHARE OF LESS-THAN-noteworthy characteristics. He was a womanizer and a heavy drinker. He bribed officials and was a member of the German Nazi Party. But buried in the dark of his heart was a diamond of compassion for the condemned Jews of Kraków, Poland.

The ones Hitler sought to kill, Schindler sought to save. He couldn't save them all, but he could save a few, and so he did what he could. What began as a factory for profit became a haven for eleven hundred fortunate souls whose names found their way onto his list—Schindler's list.

If you saw the movie by the same name, you'll remember how the story ends. With the defeat of the Nazis came the reversal of roles. Now Schindler would be hunted and the prisoners would be free. Oskar Schindler prepares to slip into the night. As he walks to his car, his factory workers line both sides of the road. They have come to thank the man who saved them. One of the Jews presents Schindler with a letter signed by each person, documenting his deed. He is also given a ring, formed out of the gold extracted from a worker's tooth. On it is carved a verse from the Talmud, "He who saves a single life saves the world entire."

In that moment, in the brisk air of the Polish night, Schindler is surrounded by the liberated. Row after row of faces. Husbands with wives. Parents with children. They know what Schindler did for them. They will never forget.

What thoughts raced through Schindler's mind in that moment? What emotions surface when a person finds himself face-to-face with lives he's changed?

Someday you'll find out. Schindler saw the faces of the delivered; you will too. Schindler heard the gratitude of the redeemed; you'll hear the same. He stood in a community of rescued souls; the same is reserved for you.

When will this occur? It will occur when Christ comes. The promise of 1 Thessalonians 2:19 isn't limited to the apostle Paul. I'll explain. "You are our hope, our joy, and the crown we will take pride in when our Lord Jesus Christ comes" (1 Thess. 2:19).

It's been about six months since Paul left Thessalonica. He, Timothy, and Silas spent three fruitful weeks in the city. The result of their stay was a nucleus of believers. Luke provides a one-sentence profile of the church when he writes: "Some of them [the Jews] were convinced and joined Paul and Silas, along with many of the Greeks who worshiped God and many of the important women" (Acts 17:4).

An eclectic group attended the first church service: Some were Jews, some were Greeks, some were influential females, but all were convinced that Jesus was the Messiah. And in a short time, all paid a price for their belief. Literally. The young believers were dragged into the presence of the city leaders and forced to post bond for their own release. That night they helped Paul, Timothy, and Silas sneak out of the city.

Paul moves on, but part of his heart is still in Thessalonica. The little church is so young, so fragile, but oh-so-special. Just the thought of them makes him proud. He longs to see them again. "We always thank God for all of you and mention you when we pray" (1 Thess. 1:2). He dreams of the day he might see them again and, even more, dreams of the day they see Christ together.

Note what he says to them: "You are our hope, our joy, and the crown we will take pride in when our Lord Jesus Christ comes" (1 Thess. 2:19). The verse conjures up an image akin to the one of Schindler and the survivors. An encounter between those freed and the one who led them to freedom. A moment in which those saved can meet the one who led them to salvation.

In this case Paul will meet with the Thessalonians. He will search the sea of faces for his friends. They will find him, and he will find them. And, in the presence of Christ, they will enjoy an eternal reunion.

Try to imagine doing the same. Think about the day Christ comes. There you are in the great circle of the redeemed. Your body has been made new—no more pain or problems. Your mind has been made new—what you once understood in part, you now understand clearly. You feel no fear, no danger, no sorrow. Though you are one of a throng, it's as if you and Jesus are all alone.

And he asks you this question. I'm speculating now, but I wonder if Christ might say these words to you: "I'm so proud that you let me use you. Because of you, others are here today. Would you like to meet them?"

Chances are you'd be surprised at such a statement. It's one thing for the apostle Paul to hear such words. He was an apostle. We can imagine a foreign missionary or famous evangelist hearing these words—but us?

Most of us wonder what influence we have. (Which is good, for if we knew, we might grow arrogant.) Most of us can relate to the words of Matthew 25, "Master, what are you talking about?" (v. 37 MSG).

At that point Jesus might—again, these are wild speculations— but Jesus might turn to the crowd and invite them. With his hand on your shoulder, he announces, "Do we have any here who were influenced by this child of mine?" One by one, they begin to step out and walk forward.

The first is your neighbor, a crusty old sort who lived next door. To be frank, you didn't expect to see him. "You never knew I was watching," he explains, "but I was. And because of you, I am here."

And then comes a cluster of people, a half dozen or so. One speaks for the others and says, "You helped out with the youth devotional when we were kids. You didn't open your mouth much, but you opened your house. We became Christians in your living room."

The line continues. A coworker noticed how you controlled your temper. A receptionist remarks how you greeted her each morning.

Someone you don't even remember reminds you of the time you saw her in the hospital. You came to visit a friend in the next bed, but on the way out you stopped and spoke a word of hope with this stranger who looked lonely.

You are most amazed by the people from other countries. After all, you never even traveled to Asia or Africa or Latin America, but look! Cambodians, Nigerians, Colombians. How did you influence them? Christ reminds you of the missionaries who came your way. Your friends said you had a soft spot for them. You always gave money. "I can't go, but I can send," you'd say. Now you understand; you didn't have a soft spot. You had the Holy Spirit. And because you were obedient to the Spirit, Utan from Cambodia wants to say thanks. So does Kinsley from Nigeria and Maria from Colombia.

It's not long before you and your Savior are encircled by the delightful collection of souls you've touched. Some you know, most you don't, but for each you feel the same. You feel what Paul felt for the Thessalonians: pride. You understand what he meant when he said: "You are our hope, our joy, and the crown we will take pride in when our Lord Jesus Christ comes" (1 Thess. 2:19).

Not a haughty, look-what-I've-done pride. But rather an awe-struck joy which declares, "I'm so proud of your faith."

But Jesus isn't finished. He loves to save the best for last, and I can't help but imagine him doing the same in heaven. You've seen the neighbors, the coworkers, the people you hardly knew, the foreigners you never knew, but there is one more group. And Jesus parts the crowd so you will see them.

Your family.

Your spouse is the first to embrace you. There were times when you wondered if either of you would make it. But now you hear the words whispered in your ear, "Thanks for not giving up on me."

Then your parents. No longer frail like you last saw them, but robust and renewed. "We're proud of you," they say. Next come your children. Children for whom you cared and over whom you prayed. They thank you; over and over they thank you. They know how hard it was, and how hard you tried, and they thank you.

And then some faces you don't recognize. You have to be told— these are grandchildren and great-grandchildren and descendants you never saw until today. They, like the others, thank you for an inherited legacy of faith.

They thank you.

Will such a moment occur? I don't know. If it does, you can be certain of two things. First, its grandeur and glory will far outstrip any description these words can carry. "No one has ever imagined what God has prepared for those who love him" (1 Cor. 2:9). And that "no one" certainly includes this one.

Second, if such a moment of reunion occurs, you can be certain you won't regret any sacrifice you made for the kingdom. The hours of service for Christ? You won't regret them. The money you gave? You'd give it a thousand times over. The times you helped the poor and loved the lost? You'd do it again.

Oskar Schindler would have. Earlier we wondered about Schindler's final thoughts. We wondered how he felt, surrounded by the people he had saved. His last appearance in the movie gives us a good idea. There, in the presence of the survivors, he tucks the letter away in his coat. He accepts the ring, and looks from face to face. For the first time, he shows emotion. He leans toward Isaac Stern, the factory foreman, and says something in a voice so low, Stern asks him to repeat it. He does. "I could have done more," he says, gesturing toward a car he could have sold. "That would have released ten prisoners." The gold pin on his lapel would have bribed an official to release two more. In that moment, Schindler's life is reduced to one value. Profit is forgotten. The factory doesn't matter. All the tears and tragedy of the nightmare are distilled into one truth. People. Only one thing counts—people.

I suggest you'll feel the same. Oh, you won't feel the regrets. Heaven knows no regret. Our God is too kind to let us face the opportunities we missed. But he is happy to let us see the ones we seized. In that moment, when you see the people God let you love, I dare say, you'd do it all again in a heartbeat.

You'd change the diapers, fix the cars, prepare the lessons, repair the roofs. One look into the faces of the ones you love, and you'd do it all again.

In a heartbeat . . . a heavenly heartbeat.

NINE

THE LAST DAY OF EVIL

A Day of Reckoning

Satan, who tricked them [God's people], was thrown into the lake of burning sulfur with the beast and the false prophet. There they will be punished day and night forever and ever.

REVELATION 20:10

MY THEATER CAREER PEAKED WHEN I WAS NINE YEARS old. I was a proud member of the Odessa Boys Choir, a collection of thirty West Texas pre-puberty kids whose primary task was to sing at ladies' luncheons and Lions Club meetings. We always wore green blazers and black slacks and marched onto the risers singing "Hey, Look Me Over." Lawrence Welk would have been proud.

Our big break came during my second year in the choir. The local junior college drama department needed some youngsters to be the Munchkins in their production of *The Wizard of Oz*. Would we be interested? *Interested* was not the word. We were thrilled. So long, Women's Wednesday Auxiliary. Hell-o-o-o-o-o, Broadway!

But our little Munchkin feet never touched the stage until the dress rehearsal. We rehearsed in a different time and place. We in the choir learned our part independently of the junior college cast. We never saw Dorothy. We never heard about the Scarecrow, and we certainly knew nothing about the Wizard.

This was significant because I was unacquainted with the plot. You assumed that everyone knew the Yellow Brick Road story? Not me. As I was growing up, *The Wizard of Oz* was on television once a year, always on a Sunday night. The rest of my friends, the rest of the school—yea verily, the rest of the free world—got to stay home and watch *The Wizard of Oz*. But did I? No, siree. Not me. No way. We had church on Sunday nights and I had to go listen to some dumb preacher . . . (Oops, sorry. Guess I tapped into some repressed childhood anger.)

Suffice it to say, I had heard of *The Wizard of Oz* but had never seen it. So I didn't know the story. On the day of the dress rehearsal, I was woefully misinformed. Since we'd practiced away from the cast, I thought we (the Odessa Boys Choir) were the cast. Oh, I'd heard the director speak of supporting characters, but I assumed that they were minor and we were major. The city of Odessa, Texas, in other words, was turning out en masse to see we Munchkins. And not just we Munchkins, but especially "me Munchkin."

You see, I'm trying to find a way to say this humbly (it is hard)—I was a special Munchkin. I was a part of the "Lullaby Guild." Some of you connoisseurs of fine movies remember there were two choruses within the larger chorus of Munchkins. There were the "Lollipop Guild" and the "Lullaby Guild." With great talent we, the other three Munchkins and myself, stepped forth at the appropriate time, presented the Kansas farm girl with a gift, and sang, "On behalf of the Lullaby Guild, we wish to welcome you to Munchkin Land."

Prior to dress rehearsal, our practice never went any further. Consequently, I knew of nothing more. I assumed that the play ended with my presentation of the gift. Many nights I fell asleep envisioning Dorothy swooning at my feet and the crowd calling for more of Max the Munchkin. Agents would call, Hollywood would beckon, Broadway would beg. My career would be launched.

Imagine, then, my chagrin when I learned the truth. Finally, we were on the real stage with the real cast. We sang our Lullaby Guild song, but rather than practice curtain calls, the director patted our heads and hurried us out of the way with, "Nice job, little Munchkins." I was stunned. "You mean there is more to the show than me?" There was, and I was about to see it.

Out of a puff of smoke came the cackle of a wicked witch. She ran from stage right to stage left, cape flying and wand waving. I went from hurt to horrified! Talk about stage fright. They didn't have to tell me to act afraid. Who said anything about a witch?! I didn't know anything about a witch!

I would have, of course, if I had known the story.

By the way, we can make the same mistake in life that I made on stage. If we aren't acquainted with the end of the script, we can grow fearful in the play. That's why it's wise to ponder the last act.

The presence of Satan is one reason some people fear the return of Christ. Understandably so. Terms such as "Armageddon," "lake of fire," and the "scarlet beast" are enough to unnerve the stoutest heart. And certainly those who do not know God have reason to be anxious. But those dressed in Christ? No. They need only read the manuscript's final reference to the devil. "Satan, who tricked them [God's people], was thrown into the lake of burning sulfur with the beast and the false prophet. There they will be punished day and night forever and ever" (Rev. 20:10).

God hasn't kept the ending a secret. He wants us to see the big picture. He wants us to know that he wins. And he also wants us to know that the evil we witness on the stage of life is not as mighty as we might think.

Many passages teach these truths, but my favorite is a couple of verses recorded by Luke. Jesus speaks the words on the night before his death. He is in the Upper Room with his followers. They are shocked to hear his prophecy that one of them will betray the Master. Their defensiveness leads to an argument, and the argument leads Jesus to exhort them to servanthood.

Then in an abrupt shift, Jesus turns to Simon Peter and makes this intriguing statement: "Simon, Simon, Satan has asked to test all of you as a farmer sifts his wheat. I have prayed that you will not lose your faith! Help your brothers be stronger when you come back to me" (Luke 22:31–32).

This passage gives us a glimpse into an unseen world. It raises many questions, but it also affords many assurances, the chief of which is the chain of command. God is clearly in control, and the devil is on a short leash. Did you notice the verb that followed Satan's name? *Ask.* "Satan has asked . . ."

The devil didn't demand, resolve, or decide. He asked. Just as he requested permission to tempt Job, he requested permission to tempt Simon Peter. Sort of recasts our image of the old snake, doesn't it? Instead of the mighty Darth Vader of Gloom, a better caricature is a skinny, back-alley punk who acts tough, but ducks fast when God flexes. "Uh, uh . . . I'd . . . uh . . . like to do a number on Peter—that is, if you don't mind." The chain of command is clear. Satan does nothing outside of God's domain, and God uses Satan to advance the cause of his kingdom.[1]

Why don't we ask someone who knows?

Julie Lindsey was working the late shift at a hotel just south of Montgomery, Alabama. Her part-time employment helped pay her college bills as she finished school. She was a devout believer. But her belief was tested the night two men held a gun to her head and forced her into their truck. She was robbed, repeatedly raped, and left handcuffed to a tree. It was two o'clock in the morning before she was rescued.

The nightmare nearly destroyed her. She couldn't function, the hotel fired her, and she dropped out of school. In her words, she was "shattered, lost, and bewildered."

This is one of the pieces that doesn't fit the puzzle. How does such a tragedy have a place in God's plan? In time, Julie learned the answer to that question. Listen to her words:

> After this experience, I spent a great deal of time thinking about God. . . . I searched and I prayed for understanding. I longed to be healed. . . . My spirit and faith were sorely tested; my spiritual journey in the months that followed was painful, but also wonderful.
>
> God allowed me to profit from an awful and devastating event. So many good things are in my life now. I have wonderful friends—most of whom I would never have met or known were it not for this experience. I have a job that allows me to work with and serve crime victims. I have a deeper relationship with God. I am spiritually wiser and more mature. I have been blessed beyond what I can tell in these pages, and I am very grateful. Romans 8:28 came alive in my life: "All things work together for good for those who love God and are called according to his purpose. . . ." Now I ask you, who won?[2]

Julie now has a ministry speaking to groups about God's mercy and healing. Can't you imagine the devil groaning with each message? What he intended for evil, God used for good. Satan unknowingly advanced the cause of the Kingdom. Rather than destroy a disciple, he strengthened a disciple.

Think about that the next time evil flaunts its cape and races across your stage. Remember, the final act has already been scripted. And the day Christ comes will be the end of evil.

In the meantime—while we wait for Christ's return—we can be encouraged because:

Jesus is praying for us. This is no ho-hum warning Peter hears from the lips of Jesus. "Simon, Simon, Satan has asked to test all of you as a farmer sifts his wheat" (Luke 22:31). Loose translation? "Satan is going to slap your faith like a farmer slaps wheat on the threshing floor." You'd expect Jesus' next words to be, "So get out of town!" Or "Duck!" or "Put it in high gear before it's too late!"

But Jesus shows no panic. He is surprisingly casual. "I have prayed that you will not lose your faith! Help your brothers be stronger when you come back to me" (v. 32).

Can you hear the calmness in his voice? Forgive me, but I almost detect the accent of a streetwise, tattooed, leather-jacketed guy from Brooklyn: "Yo, Peter, Satan wanted to kill you, but you don't need to worry. I told him to go easy."

The sum of the matter is simple: Jesus has spoken and Satan has listened. The devil may land a punch or two. He may even win a few rounds, but he never wins the fight. Why? Because Jesus takes up for you. You'll love the way this truth appears in Hebrews: "But because Jesus lives forever, he will never stop serving as priest. So he is able always to save those who come to God through him because he always lives, asking God to help them" (Heb. 7:24–25).

Here's how it reads in other translations:

"He always lives to intercede for them" (NIV).

"He is always living to plead on their behalf" (NEB).

"He's . . . always on the job to speak up for them" (MSG).

Paul says the same thing in Romans: "The Spirit himself speaks to God for us, even begs God for us" (Rom. 8:26). And then in verse 34, "The One who died for us—who was raised to life for us!—is in the presence of God at this very moment sticking up for us" (MSG).

Jesus, at this very moment, is protecting you. You may feel like a Munchkin on stage with a wicked witch, but don't worry. Evil must pass through Christ before it can touch you. And God will "never let you be pushed past your limit; he'll always be there to help you come through it" (1 Cor. 10:13 MSG).

"The Lord knows how to rescue godly men from trials" (2 Peter 2:9 NIV), and he will rescue you. He will rescue us all on the day Christ comes.

We can be encouraged because Jesus is praying for us. We can also be encouraged because:

We will prevail. "When you come back to me . . ." are the words Jesus uses with Peter. Not "*if* you come back to me," or "at the *possibility* you'll come back to me," but "*when* you come back to me." Jesus has absolutely no insecurity, and neither should we. What Jesus did with Peter is what I wish someone had done with me, the Munchkin. He read him the rest of the script.

Suppose you had been present during that dress rehearsal of *The Wizard of Oz*. Suppose you'd seen a wide-eyed, red-headed kid hiding from the witch. And suppose you felt sorry for him. What would you have done? How would you have made him feel better?

Simple, you would have told him the rest of the story. "Sure, Max, the witch stirs up some trouble. Yes, Dorothy and the guys have their problems. But in the end, the witch melts like wax and everyone gets home safely."

Isn't that what God has told us about Satan? Read again the words of John: "The Devil who deceived them [God's people] will be hurled into Lake Fire and Brimstone, joining the Beast and False Prophet, the three in torment around the clock for ages without end" (Rev. 20:10 MSG).

God has kept no secrets. He has told us that, while on this yellow brick road, we will experience trouble. Disease will afflict bodies. Divorce will break hearts. Death will make widows and devastation will destroy countries. We should not expect any less. But just because the devil shows up and cackles, we needn't panic. "In [this] world you will have tribulation," Jesus promises, "but be of good cheer, I have overcome the world" (John 16:33 NKJV).

Our Master speaks of an accomplished deed. "I *have* overcome the world." It is finished. The battle is over. Be alert. But don't be alarmed. The witch has no power. The manuscript has been published. The book has been bound. Satan is loosed for a season, but the season is oh-so-brief. The devil knows this. "He is filled with fury, because he knows that his time is short" (Rev. 12:12 NIV). Just a few more scenes, just a few more turns in the road, and his end will come.

And we Munchkins will be there to see it.

TEN

ITEMIZED GRACE

A Day of Permanent Pardon

*In those days before the flood, people were eating and drinking,
marrying and giving their children to be married, until the day
Noah entered the boat. They knew nothing about what was
happening until the flood came and destroyed them. It will be the
same when the Son of Man comes.*

MATTHEW 24:38–39

DENALYN AND I RECENTLY SPENT HALF A SATURDAY
watching our daughter Andrea play in a middle school volleyball
tournament. The first game was at eight o'clock and the second
at eleven o'clock. In between the two contests, one of the parents
invited the rest of us parents to eat breakfast at her restaurant.
Not "a" restaurant, but "her" restaurant. Not wanting to miss a
free meal, a dozen or so of us piled into our cars and off we went.

The food was served cafeteria style, so we all stood in line.
All, that is, except our hostess. She stood next to the cash register.

Being the owner, she wanted to make sure we didn't pay for our food. The attendant totaled the bill and rang up the charge, but we never gave a penny. As each of us took our turn before the register, our generous friend would tell the attendant, "I know him, he's with me. His bill is covered." Ah, the joy of knowing the right person.

Consider what happened that morning. The kindness of our hostess was magnified. Every time a debt was pardoned, her generosity was revealed. Also, those who knew the hostess were rewarded. Our trays were full and soon were our bellies. Why? Well, we simply accepted her invitation. And, those who did not know her had to pay the price. Though her generosity was abundant, it was not universal.

It may seem odd to hear someone analyze a breakfast invitation. Either I am hinting for another breakfast, or I am about to make a point. Actually, I'm going to make a point (though breakfast sounds good). What we saw that Saturday morning is a sampling of what we will all see when Christ comes.

The day Christ comes will be a day of judgment. This judgment will be marked by three accomplishments.

First, God's grace will be revealed. Our host will receive all the credit and attention.

Second, rewards for his servants will be unveiled. Those who accepted his invitation will be uniquely honored.

And third, those who do not know him will pay a price. A severe, terrible price. Jesus refers to this price in Matthew 24:38–39: "In those days before the flood, people were eating and drinking, marrying and giving their children to be married, until the day Noah entered the boat. They knew nothing about what was happening until the flood came and destroyed them. It will be the same when the Son of Man comes."

As Jesus sought for a way to explain his return, he hearkened back to the flood of Noah. Parallels are obvious. A message of judgment was proclaimed then. It is proclaimed still. People didn't listen then. They refuse to listen today. Noah was sent to save the faithful. Christ was sent to do the same. A flood of water came then. A flood of fire will come next. Noah built a safe place out of wood. Jesus made a safe place with the cross. Those who believed hid in the ark. Those who believe are hidden in Christ.

Most important, what God did in Noah's generation, he will do at Christ's return. He will pronounce a universal, irreversible judgment. A judgment in which grace is revealed, rewards are unveiled, and the impenitent are punished. As you read the story of Noah, you won't find the word *judgment*. But you will find ample evidence of one.

The era of Noah was a sad one. "People on earth did what God said was evil, and violence was everywhere" (Gen. 6:11). Such rebellion broke the heart of God. "His heart was filled with pain" (Gen. 6:6). He sent a flood, a mighty purging flood, upon the earth. The skies rained for forty days. "The water rose so much that even the highest mountains under the sky were covered by it. It continued to rise until it was more than twenty feet above the mountains" (Gen. 7:19–20). Only Noah, his family, and the animals on the ark escaped. Everyone else perished. God didn't slam the gavel on the bench, but he did close the door of the ark. According to Jesus: "It will be the same when the Son of Man comes" (Matt. 24:39). And so a judgment was rendered.

Talk about a thought that stirs anxiety! Just the term *judgment day* conjures up images of tiny people at the base of a huge bench. On the top of the bench is a book and behind the bench is God and from God comes a voice of judgment—Guilty! *Gulp.* We are supposed to encourage each other with these words? How can the judgment stir anything except panic? For the unprepared, it can't. But for the follower of Jesus who understands the judgment—the hour is not to be dreaded. In fact, once we understand it, we can anticipate it.

Let's deal with some fundamental questions, and I'll show you what I mean.

Who will be judged? Everyone who has ever lived. According to Matthew 25:32, "Before him [the Son of Man] will be gathered all the nations" (RSV). In 2 Corinthians 5:10 Paul writes, "For we must all appear before the judgment seat of Christ" (NIV). Just as the whole earth was judged in the days of Noah, all humanity will be judged on the day Christ comes.

This stirs a hornet's nest of dilemmas, not the least of which is: What of those who never heard of Christ? What of those who lived before the time of Christ or who never heard his gospel? Will they be judged as well? Yes, but by a different standard.

Men will be judged on the basis of the light they had, not on the basis of a light they never saw. The person in the remote jungle who never heard of Jesus is judged differently than the person who is only a broadcast or open Bible away from the gospel.

Jesus explains as much with his harsh criticism of the cities Chorazin and Bethsaida:

> In the towns where Jesus had worked most of his miracles, the people refused to turn to God. So Jesus was upset with them and said: "You people of Chorazin are in for trouble! You people of Bethsaida are in for trouble too! If the miracles that took place in your towns had happened in Tyre and Sidon, the people there would have turned to God long ago. They would have dressed in sackcloth and put ashes on their heads. I tell you that on the day of judgment the people of Tyre and Sidon will get off easier than you will." (Matt. 11:20–22 CEV)

The phrase "get off easier" is a revealing one. Not everyone will be judged by the same standard. The greater our privilege, the greater our responsibilities. Chorazin and Bethsaida saw much, so much was expected of them. The gospel was clearly presented to them, yet they clearly rejected it. "The saddest road to hell is that which runs under the pulpit, past the Bible and through the midst of warnings and invitations."[1]

On the other hand, Tyre and Sidon saw less, so less was expected. They, to use the words of Christ, will "get off easier" than others.

The principle? God's judgment is based upon humanity's response to the message received. He will never hold us accountable for what he doesn't tell us.

At the same time, he will never let us die without telling us something. Even those who never heard of Christ are given a message about the character of God. "The heavens declare the glory of God; the skies proclaim the work of his hands. Day after day they pour forth speech; night after night they display knowledge. There is no speech or language where their voice is not heard" (Ps. 19:1–3 NIV).

Nature is God's first missionary. Where there is no Bible, there are sparkling stars. Where there are no preachers, there are springtimes. Where there is no testament of Scripture, there is the testament of changing seasons and breath-stealing sunsets. If a person has nothing but nature, then nature is enough to reveal something about God. As Paul says: "The basic reality of God is plain enough. Open your eyes and there it is! By taking a long and thoughtful look at what God has created, people have always been able to see what their eyes as such can't see: eternal power, for instance, and the mystery of his divine being" (Rom. 1:19–20 MSG).

Paul goes on to say, "God's law is not something alien, imposed on us from without, but woven into the very fabric of our creation. There is something deep within them that echoes God's yes and no, right and wrong. Their response to God's yes and no will become public knowledge on the day God makes his final decision about every man and woman. The Message from God that I proclaim through Jesus Christ takes into account all these differences" (Rom. 2:15–16 MSG).

We do not know how God will take the differences into account, but he will. If you and I, in our sinful state, are concerned about it, we can be sure that God in his holiness has already settled it. We can trust the witnesses who cry from heaven: "Yes, Lord God All-Powerful, your judgments are honest and fair" (Rev. 16:7 CEV).

Having established who will be judged, let's ask another question.

What will be judged? Simply put: all things that we have done in this present life. Again 2 Corinthians 5:10 is clear: "For we must all appear before the judgment seat of Christ, that each one may receive what is due him for the things done while in the body, whether good or bad" (NIV). This includes deeds, words, and thoughts. Isn't that the understanding of Revelation 20:12? "The dead were judged by what they had done, which was written in the books." Similar statements are found elsewhere.

"God will bring every deed into judgment, including every hidden thing, whether it is good or evil" (Eccles. 12:14 NIV).

"On the day of judgment men will render account for every careless word they utter" (Matt. 12:36 RSV).

Jesus summarizes the matter in Luke 12:2: "Everything that is hidden will be shown, and everything that is secret will be made known."

Even for the believer? Will we be judged as well? Hebrews

10:30 states as much: "The Lord will judge his people" (NIV). The apostle Paul concurs: "For we will all stand before God's judgment seat. . . . So then, each of us will give an account of himself to God" (Rom. 14:10, 12 NIV).

Did I detect an eyebrow arching? Why would a Christian be judged? Not a bad question. Let's make it our third.

Why will Christians be judged? Don't we have a new wardrobe? Aren't we clothed in the righteousness of Christ? Haven't our sins been cast as far as the east is from the west? They have. And we can stand firmly on this underpinning truth: "Therefore, there is now no condemnation for those who are in Christ Jesus" (Rom. 8:1 NIV). Because we are clothed in Christ, we can be without fear on the day God judges us.

But if we are clothed in Christ, why do we need a judgment at all?

I can find at least two answers. First, so our rewards can be unveiled, and second, so that God's grace can be revealed.

Let's talk for a moment about rewards. Salvation is the result of grace. Without exception, no man or woman has ever done one work to enhance the finished work of the cross. Our service does not earn our salvation. Our service does, however, impact our rewards. As one writer stated, "We are accepted into heaven on the basis of faith alone, but we are adorned in heaven on the basis of the fruits of our faith."[2]

If this strikes you as strange, you aren't alone. Scripture offers just enough teaching to convince us of rewards, but not enough to answer our questions about them. In what form do they come? How are they dispensed? We aren't told. We are simply assured they exist. In addition to the crowns of life, righteousness, and glory, Scripture indicates that there are other rewards.

Some of the clearest writing on the topic is found in 1 Corinthians 3:10–15. In these verses, Paul envisions two lives. Both are built on the foundation of Christ; that is to say, both are saved. One, however, adds to that foundation with valuable works of gold, silver, and jewels. The other is content to take the cheap route and makes no substantive contribution to the kingdom. His work is comprised of flammable wood, grass, and straw.

On the day of judgment, the nature of each work will be revealed. Paul writes: "That Day will appear with fire, and the fire will test everyone's work to show what sort of work it was. If the building that has been put on the foundation still stands, the builder will get a reward. But if the building is burned up, the builder will suffer loss. The builder will be saved, but it will be as one who escaped from a fire" (1 Cor. 3:13–15).

Please note: Both builders will be saved, but only one will be rewarded. And that reward will be on the basis of works. Exactly what forms the rewards will take, we do not know. I was once counseled to maintain a "reverent agnosticism" on the question. Translated: be peacefully ignorant.

My feeling is that the rewards will come in the form of added responsibility, not added privilege. Such is the indication from Matthew 25:21: "Well done, good and faithful servant; you were faithful over a few things, I will make you ruler over many things. Enter into the joy of your lord" (NKJV). The worker appears to be given more duty rather than more relaxation. But again, we don't know for sure.

What we do know is this: We are saved by grace, and we are rewarded according to deeds. Anything beyond that is speculation. In fact, any speculation beyond that is dangerous lest we grow competitive.

But won't we be competitive in heaven? Won't the distribution of awards create jealousy for some and arrogance for others? No, it won't. In our sinless state our focus will finally be off of ourselves and onto Jesus Christ. We will gladly adopt the attitude Christ commands in Luke 17:10: "So you also, when you have done everything you were told to do, should say 'We are unworthy servants; we have only done our duty'" (NIV).

Still the question remains, why must our deeds be exposed? According to Jesus, "Everything that is hidden will be shown, and everything that is secret will be made known" (Luke 12:2). Is Jesus saying that all secrets will be revealed? The secrets of sinners and saints alike? He is, but—and this is essential—the sins of the saved will be revealed as *forgiven* sins. Our transgressions will be announced as *pardoned* transgressions. That is the second reason believers will be judged. The first, so our acts can be rewarded and second, so that God's grace can be revealed.

You've probably heard the story of the couple who resorted to do-it-yourself marriage counseling. They resolved to make a list of each other's faults and then read them aloud. Sounds like a constructive evening, don't you think? So she made hers and he made his. The wife gave her list of complaints to the husband and he read them aloud. "You snore, you eat in bed, you get home too late and up too early . . ." After finishing, the husband did the same. He gave her his list. But when she looked at the paper, she began to smile. He, too, had written his grievances, but next to each he had written, "I forgive this."

The result was a tabulated list of grace.

You'll receive such a list on judgment day. Remember the primary purpose of judgment: to reveal the grace of the Father. As your sins are announced, God's grace is magnified.

Imagine the event. You are before the judgment seat of Christ. The book is opened and the reading begins—each sin, each deceit, each occasion of destruction and greed. But as soon as the infraction is read, grace is proclaimed.

> Disrespected parents at age thirteen.
> Shaded the truth at age fifteen.
> Gossiped at age twenty-six.
> Lusted at age thirty.
> Disregarded the leading of the Spirit at age forty.
> Disobeyed God's Word at age fifty-two.

The result? God's merciful verdict will echo through the universe. For the first time in history, we will understand the depth of his goodness. Itemized grace. Catalogued kindness. Registered forgiveness. We will stand in awe as one sin after another is proclaimed, and then pardoned. Jealousies revealed, then removed. Infidelities announced, then cleansed. Lies exposed, then erased.

The devil will shrink back in defeat. The angels will step forward in awe. And we saints will stand tall in God's grace. As we see how much he has forgiven us, we will see how much he loves us. And we will worship him. We will join in the song of the saints: "You are worthy to take the scroll and to open its seals, because you were killed, and with the blood of your death you bought people for God from every tribe, language, people, and nation" (Rev. 5:9).

What a triumph this will be for our Master!

Perhaps you're thinking, *It will be triumph for him, but humiliation for me.* No, it won't. Scripture promises, "The one who trusts in him will never be put to shame" (1 Peter 2:6 NIV). But how can this be? If the hidden is known and the secret is shown, won't I be embarrassed beyond recovery? No, you won't. Here is why.

Shame is a child of self-centeredness. Heaven's occupants are not self-centered, they are Christ-centered. You will be in your sinless state. The sinless don't protect a reputation or project an image. You won't be ashamed. You'll be happy to let God do in heaven what he did on earth—be honored in your weaknesses.

Heads bowed in shame? No. Heads bowed in worship? No doubt.

By the way, won't it feel good to have it all out in the open?

No more games. No more make-believe. No more cover-ups. No more status seekers or ladder climbers. The result will be the first genuine community of forgiven people. Only one is worthy of the applause of heaven, and he's the one with the pierced hands and feet.

So don't worry about feeling shame. The believer has nothing to fear from the judgment. The unbeliever, however, has much to fear. Which takes us to our final question.

What is the destiny of those who don't know Christ? Remember the three purposes of judgment? God's grace will be revealed. His rewards will be unveiled. And those who do not know him will pay a price. A severe, terrible price.

Let's return to the story of the free meal at the restaurant. What would have happened if a stranger tried to horn in on the breakfast? No one did, but someone could have tried. He could have slipped in between the invited guests and acted like he was a part of the group. Would he have succeeded? Would he have fooled our hostess? No. She knew all her guests by name.

So does Christ. "The Lord knows those who belong to him" (2 Tim. 2:19). Just as our hostess stood next to the cash register, so our Savior will stand at the judgment seat. Just as she covered our debt, so Christ will forgive our sins. And just as she would have turned away the ones she did not know, Jesus will do the same. "I don't know this person," she would have said. "Get away from me, you who do evil. I never knew you," Jesus will declare (Matt. 7:23).

For that person, the day of judgment will be a day of shame. His sins will be revealed, but not as forgiven sins. Can you imagine the same list minus the proclamation of pardon? One deed after another until not even the sinner questions God's right to punish. For those who never accepted God's mercy, judgment will be a day of wrath. It will be like it was in the days of Noah. But that is a topic for the next page.

Eleven

Love's Caution

A Day of Ultimate Justice

> *The flood came and destroyed them. It will be the same when the Son of Man comes.*
>
> MATTHEW 24:39

I DID SOMETHING DIFFERENT RECENTLY; I LISTENED TO the airline attendant as she gave her warnings. Typically, my nose is buried in a book or project, but a commercial plane had crashed the day before. Watching the newscasts of the event convinced me to pay attention. I realized that if this plane had trouble, I wouldn't know what to do.

So I listened. As she held up the seat belt, I buckled mine. As she described the oxygen mask, I looked up to see where it was stored. When she pointed toward the exit doors, I turned to find them. That's when I noticed what she notices on every flight. No one was listening! No one was paying attention. I was shocked. I seriously considered standing up and shouting, "You folks better listen up. One mishap and this plane becomes a flaming mausoleum. What this woman is telling you might save your life!"

I wondered what would happen if she used more drastic means. What if she took a gasoline-drenched doll and set it on fire? What if the in-flight screen projected images of passengers racing to exit a blazing plane? What if she marched up and down the aisle, yanking away newspapers and snatching up magazines, demanding that the passengers listen if they want to survive this flaming inferno?

She would lose her job. But she'd make her point. And she'd also be doing the passengers a favor. Our Savior has done the same for us. He was motivated by more than duty, however. He was motivated by love. And love cautions the loved.

Christ's caution is clear: "In those days before the flood, people were eating and drinking, marrying and giving their children to be married, until the day Noah entered the boat. They knew nothing about what was happening until the flood came and destroyed them. It will be the same when the Son of Man comes" (Matt. 24:38–39).

As we pointed out in the last chapter, the parallels between the flood of Noah and the return of Christ come easily. People refused to listen then. Many refuse to listen still. God sent a safe place for the faithful then: an ark. God sends a safe place for the faithful today: his Son. A flood came then. A flood will come. The first was a flood of water. The next is a flood of vengeance. The first flood was irreversible. So is the second. Once the door is shut, it is shut forever. There was screaming on the day of the flood. There will be "weeping and gnashing of teeth" on the day of judgment (Matt. 25:30 NIV). Regarding the lost, the Bible says, "The smoke of their torment goes up for ever and ever; and they have no rest, day or night" (Rev. 14:11 RSV).

This is serious business. Hell is a serious topic. A topic we'd rather avoid. We agree with C. S. Lewis: "There is no doctrine which I would more willingly remove from Christianity than [hell], if it lay in my power. . . . I would pay any price to be able to say truthfully: 'All will be saved.'"[1]

Wouldn't we all? But dare we? Let's work with this for a moment.

Does hell serve a purpose? As much as we resist the idea, isn't the absence of hell even worse? Remove it from the Bible and, at the same time, remove any notion of a just God and a trustworthy Scripture. Let me explain.

If there is no hell, God is not just. If there is no punishment of sin, heaven is apathetic toward the rapists and pillagers and mass murderers of society. If there is no hell, God is blind toward the victims and has turned his back on those who pray for relief. If there is no wrath toward evil, then God is not love, for love hates that which is evil.

To say there is no hell is also to say God is a liar and his Scripture untrue. The Bible repeatedly and stoutly affirms the dualistic outcome of history. Some will be saved. Some will be lost. "Many of those who sleep in the dust of the earth shall awake, some to everlasting life, and some to shame and everlasting contempt" (Dan.

12:2 RSV). Paul agreed: "To those who by patience in well-doing seek for glory and honor and immortality, he will give eternal life; but for those who are factious and do not obey the truth, but obey wickedness, there will be wrath and fury" (Rom. 2:7–8 RSV).

People object to this point by gravitating to the teachings of Jesus. The idea of hell, they say, is an Old Testament idea. Curiously, the Old Testament is comparatively silent on the topic. The New Testament is the primary storehouse of thoughts on hell. And Jesus is the primary teacher. No one spoke of eternal punishment more often or more clearly than Christ himself.

Think about these facts: Thirteen percent of the teachings of Christ are about judgment and hell. More than half of his parables relate to God's eternal judgment of sinners. Of the twelve times that the word *gehenna*—the strongest biblical word for hell—appears in Scripture, there is only one time in which Jesus was not the speaker.[2] No one spoke of hell more than Christ did. "Anyone who believes and is baptized will be saved, but anyone who does not believe will be punished" (Mark 16:16).

Are we to ignore these statements? Can we scissor them out of our Bibles? Only at the expense of a just God and a reliable Bible. Hell is a very real part of the economy of heaven.

Even now, before Christ comes, the presence of hell serves a powerful purpose. It functions somewhat like my dad's workshop. That is where he disciplined my brother and me. When my mom was angry, we got spankings. When my dad was angry, we got whippings. You can guess which one we preferred. All Dad had to say was, "Go to the workshop," and my bottom would begin to tingle. I don't know how you feel about corporal punishment. I don't mention the topic to discuss it. I mention it to explain the impact that the workshop had on my behavior.

You see, my father loved me. I knew he loved me. And most of the time, his love was enough. There were many bad things I didn't do because I knew he loved me. But there were a few times when love was not enough. The temptation was so strong, or the rebellion so fierce, that the thought of his love didn't slow me down. But the thought of his anger did. When love didn't compel me, fear corrected me. The thought of the workshop—and the weeping and gnashing of teeth therein—was just enough to straighten me out.

The application might be obvious. If not, let me make it so. Our heavenly Father loves his children. He really does. Most of the time, that love will be enough to make us follow him. But there will be times when it won't. The lure of lust will be so mighty, the magnet of greed so strong, the promise of power so seductive, that people will reject the love of God. In those moments, the Holy Spirit may mention "the workshop." He may remind us that "whatever a man sows, that he will also reap" (Gal. 6:7 RSV). And the reminder that there is a place of punishment may be just what we need to correct our behavior.

Jesus provides such a reminder in Luke 16.

What is hell like? Jesus is the only eyewitness of hell who has walked on earth. And his description stands as the most reliable

and graphic ever written. Every single word in this story is significant. Every single word is sobering.

> There was a rich man who always dressed in the finest clothes
> and lived in luxury every day. And a very poor man named
> Lazarus, whose body was covered with sores, was laid at the
> rich man's gate. He wanted to eat only the small pieces of food
> that fell from the rich man's table. And the dogs would come
> and lick his sores. (Luke 16:19–21)

The story begins at a posh house in an exclusive neighborhood.
The man who owns the house is extravagant. He wears the finest
clothes. The Greek suggests he uses fabric that is literally worth
its weight in gold. He eats sumptuously every day. In an era when
most can afford meat once a week, his daily diet is exotic.

Botanical gardens sprawl within his gates. Gold and china
sparkle upon his table. Ripe fruit from groomed orchards are a
part of each meal. He lives, Jesus says, in luxury every day.

But outside his gate sits a beggar by the name of Lazarus. His
body is covered with sores. Skin drapes from his bones. He's been
laid at the gate. Someone too kind to ignore him, yet too power-
less to help him, loaded the man in a wagon and deposited him in
front of the house of the rich man. In those days the wealthy didn't
use napkins after a meal; they would wipe their hands on chunks
of bread. Lazarus asks only for the crumbs from this bread.

Heed the contrast. A nameless baron basking in leisure. A

named beggar lying in misery. Between them a gate; a tall, spiked door. Inside a person feasts. Outside a person starves. And from above, a just God renders a verdict. The curtain of death falls. Both die. And as the stage lights are turned up on scene two, we gasp at the reversal of destiny.

"Later, Lazarus died, and the angels carried him to the arms of Abraham. The rich man died, too, and was buried. In the place of the dead, he was in much pain" (vv. 22–23).

The beggar, who had nothing but God, now has everything. The wealthy man, who had everything but God, now has nothing. The beggar, whose body probably had been cast into a garbage dump called Gehenna, is now honored with a seat near Abraham. The rich man, who'd been buried in a hewn tomb and anointed with priceless myrrh, is destined for the Gehenna of eternity. The pain of Lazarus has ended. The pain of the rich man has just begun.

If the story ceased here, we would be stunned. But the story goes on. Jesus now escorts us to the edge of hell and reveals its horrors. The rich man is in relentless torment. Five verses make four references to his pain.

"In the place of the dead, he was in much pain" (v. 23).

"I am suffering in this fire!" (v. 24).

"Now he [Lazarus] is comforted here, and you are suffering" (v. 25).

"I [the rich man] have five brothers, and Lazarus could warn them so that they will not come to this place of pain" (v. 28).

Perhaps the last phrase is the most telling. The rich man defines his new home as a "place of pain." Every fiber of his being is tortured. And what's worse (yes, there is something worse), he can see the place of comfort which he will never know. He lifts up his eyes and sees the beggar who once lived at his gate. Now the rich man is the one begging.

"The rich man saw Abraham far away with Lazarus at his side. He called, 'Father Abraham, have mercy on me! Send Lazarus to dip his finger in water and cool my tongue, because I am suffering in this fire!'" (vv. 23–24).

Hell might be tolerable if its citizens were lobotomized. But such is not the case. The citizens are awake. They ask questions. They speak. They plead. Of all the horrors of hell, the worst must be the knowledge that the suffering will never cease. "These will go away into eternal punishment, but the righteous into eternal life" (Matt. 25:46 NASB).

The same adjective used to describe the length of heavenly life is used to describe the duration of punishment: *eternal*. Good people live "forever." Evil people are punished "forever."[3]

Revelation 14:11 is equally disturbing: "The smoke from their burning pain will rise forever and ever. There will be no rest, day or night, for those who worship the beast and his idol or who get the mark of his name."

We would love to believe that sinners will be given a second chance, that a few months or millenniums of purgatory will purify their souls, and ultimately all will be saved. But as attractive as this sounds, Scripture simply doesn't teach it. Abraham's response to the lost man's request affirms that the patience of God stops at the gate of hell. "Between us and you a great chasm has been fixed, so that those who want to go from here to you cannot, nor can anyone cross over from there to us" (Luke 16:26 NIV).

The term *fixed* originates in a Greek word that means "to set forth, to make fast." It literally means "to cement, to permanently establish." Paul uses the same word in Romans 16:25 when he boasts about Jesus, "who is able to establish you" (NIV).

Fascinating. The same power that establishes the saved in the kingdom, seals the fate of the lost. There will be no missionary journeys to hell and no holiday excursions to heaven. This is a hard teaching, and it gives rise to a hard question.

How could a loving God send people to hell? That's a commonly asked question. The question itself reveals a couple of misconceptions.

First, God does not *send* people to hell. He simply honors their choice. Hell is the ultimate expression of God's high regard for the dignity of man. He has never forced us to choose him, even when that means we would choose hell. As C. S. Lewis stated: "There are only two kinds of people in the end: those who say to God, 'Thy will be done' and those to whom God says, in the end, 'Thy will be done.' All that are in hell choose it."[4] In another book Lewis said it this way: "I willingly believe the damned are, in one sense, successful rebels to the end; that the doors of hell are locked on the inside."[5]

No, God does not "send" people to hell. Nor does he send "people" to hell. That is the second misconception.

The word *people* is neutral, implying innocence. Nowhere does Scripture teach that innocent people are condemned. People do not go to hell. Sinners do. The rebellious do. The self-centered do. So how could a loving God send people to hell? He doesn't. He simply honors the choice of sinners.

Jesus' story concludes with a surprising twist. We hear the rich man plead: "Please send Lazarus to my father's house. I have five brothers, and Lazarus could warn them so that they will not come to this place of pain" (Luke 16:27–28).

What is this? The rich man suddenly possessed with evangelistic fervor? The one who never knew God now prays for missionaries? Remarkable what one step into hell can do to your priorities. Those who know the horrors of hell will do whatever it takes to warn their friends.

Jesus, who understands the final flood of wrath, pleads with us to make any sacrifice to avoid it. "If your hand or your foot causes you to sin, cut it off and throw it away; it is better for you to enter life maimed or lame than with two hands or two feet to be thrown into the eternal fire" (Matt. 18:8–9 RSV).

This story is, without a doubt, the most disturbing story Jesus ever told. It's packed with words such as *torment, pain,* and *suffering.* It teaches concepts that are tough to swallow, concepts such as "conscious punishment" and "permanent banishment." But it also teaches a vital truth that is easily overlooked. This story teaches the unimaginable love of God.

"What? The love of God? Max, you and I read two different

stories. The one I read spoke of punishment, hell, and eternal misery. How does that teach the love of God?"

Because God went there, for you. God spanned the chasm. God crossed the gulf. Why? So you won't have to.

Never forget that while on the cross, Jesus became sin. "Christ had no sin, but God made him become sin so that in Christ we could become right with God" (2 Cor. 5:21). Jesus became sin, the very object God hates, the very object God punishes.

"The wages of sin is death," Paul stated in Romans 6:23 (NIV). The rich man is testimony to the verse. Lead a life of sin and earn an eternity of suffering. God punishes sin. Even when the sin is laid on his own son. That is exactly what occurred on the cross. "The LORD has laid on him the iniquity of us all" (Isa. 53:6 NIV).

And because he did, Jesus "took our suffering on him and felt our pain for us" (Isa. 53:4). What the rich man felt, Jesus felt. What you saw as you stared into the pit of hell, Jesus experienced . . . the pain, the anguish, the isolation, the loneliness. No wonder he cried out, "My God, my God, why have you rejected me?" (Mark 15:34).

Like the rich man, Jesus knew hell. But unlike the rich man, Jesus didn't stay there. "He [Jesus] too shared in their humanity so that by his death he might destroy him who holds the power of death—that is, the devil—and free those who all their lives were held in slavery by their fear of death" (Heb. 2:14–15 NIV).

Yes, hell's misery is deep, but not as deep as God's love.

So how do we apply this message? If you are saved, it should cause you to rejoice. You've been rescued. A glance into hell leads the believer to rejoice. But it also leads the believer to redouble his efforts to reach the lost. To understand hell is to pray more earnestly and to serve more diligently. Ours is a high-stakes mission.

And the lost? What is the meaning of this message for the unprepared? Heed the warnings and get ready. This plane won't fly forever. "Death is the destiny of every man; the living should take this to heart" (Eccles. 7:2 NIV).

TWELVE

SEEING JESUS

A Day of Joyful Amazement

We know that when Christ comes again, we will be like him,
because we will see him as he really is.

1 JOHN 3:2

AUGUSTINE ONCE POSED THE FOLLOWING EXPERIMENT.
Imagine God saying to you, "I'll make a deal with you if you wish.
I'll give you anything and everything you ask: pleasure, power,
honor, wealth, freedom, even peace of mind and a good conscience. Nothing will be a sin; nothing will be forbidden; and
nothing will be impossible to you. You will never be bored and
you will never die. Only . . . you will never see my face."[1]

The first part of the proposition is appealing. Isn't there a part
of us, a pleasure-loving part of us, that perks up at the thought of
guiltless, endless delight? But then, just as we are about to raise
our hands and volunteer, we hear the final phrase, "You will never
see my face."

And we pause. *Never?* Never know the image of God? Never, ever behold the presence of Christ? At this point, tell me, doesn't the bargain begin to lose some of its appeal? Don't second thoughts begin to surface? And doesn't the test teach us something about our hearts? Doesn't the exercise reveal a deeper, better part of us that wants to see God?

For many it does.

For others, however, Augustine's exercise doesn't raise interest as much as it raises a question. An awkward question, one you may be hesitant to ask for fear of sounding naive or irreverent. Since you may feel that way, why don't I ask it for you? At the risk of putting words in your mouth, let me put words in your mouth. "Why the big deal?" you ask. "No disrespect intended. Of course I want to see Jesus. But to see him *forever!?* Will he be that amazing?"

According to Paul he will. "On the day when the Lord Jesus comes," he writes, ". . . all the people who have believed will be amazed at Jesus" (2 Thess. 1:10).

Amazed at Jesus. Not amazed at angels or mansions or new bodies or new creations. Paul doesn't measure the joy of encountering the apostles or embracing our loved ones. If we will be amazed at these, which certainly we will, he does not say. What he does say is that we will be amazed at Jesus.

What we have only seen in our thoughts, we will see with our eyes. What we've struggled to imagine, we will be free to behold. What we've seen in a glimpse, we will then see in full view. And, according to Paul, we will be amazed.

What will be so amazing?

Of course I have no way of answering that question from personal experience. But I can lead you to someone who can. One Sunday morning many Sundays ago, a man named John saw Jesus. And what he saw, he recorded, and what he recorded has tantalized seekers of Christ for two thousand years.

To envision John, we should imagine an old man with stooped shoulders and shuffling walk. The years have long past since he was a young disciple with Jesus in Galilee. His master has been crucified, and most of his friends are dead. And now, the Roman government has exiled him to the island of Patmos. Let's imagine him on the beach. He has come here to worship. The wind stirs the cattails and the waves slap the sand, and John sees nothing but water—an ocean that separates him from his home. But no amount of water could separate him from Christ.

"On the Lord's day I was in the Spirit, and I heard a loud voice behind me that sounded like a trumpet. The voice said, 'Write what you see in a book and send it to the seven churches: to Ephesus, Smyrna, Pergamum, Thyatira, Sardis, Philadelphia, and Laodicea'" (Rev. 1:10–11).

John is about to see Jesus. Of course this isn't his first time to see his Savior.

You and I only read about the hands that fed the thousands. Not John. He saw them—knuckled fingers, callused palms. He saw them. You and I only read about the feet that found a path through the waves. Not John. John saw them—sandaled, ten-toed, and dirty. You and I only read about his eyes—his flashing eyes, his fiery eyes, his weeping eyes. Not so with John. John saw them. Gazing on the crowds, dancing with laughter, searching for souls. John had seen Jesus.

For three years he'd followed Christ. But this encounter was far different from any in Galilee. The image was so vivid, the impression so powerful, John was knocked out cold. "When I saw him I fell in a dead faint at his feet" (Rev. 1:17 TJB).

He describes the event like this:

> I turned to see who was talking to me. When I turned, I saw seven golden lampstands and someone among the lampstands who was "like a Son of Man." He was dressed in a long robe and had a gold band around his chest. His head and hair were white like wool, as white as snow, and his eyes were like flames of fire. His feet were like bronze that glows hot in a furnace, and his voice was like the noise of flooding water. He held seven stars in his right hand, and a sharp double-edged sword came out of his mouth. He looked like the sun shining at its brightest time. When I saw him, I fell down at his feet like a dead man. He put his right hand on me and said, "Do not be afraid." (Rev. 1:12–17)

If you are puzzled by what you just read, you aren't alone. The world of Revelation cannot be contained or explained; it can only be pondered. And John gives us a vision to ponder, a vision of Christ that comes at you from all angles. Swords and bronze feet and white hair and sunlight. What are we to make of such an image?

First of all, keep in mind that what John wrote is not what he saw. (Yes, you read that sentence correctly.) What John wrote is not what he saw. What he wrote is *like* what he saw. But what he saw was so otherworldly that he had no words to describe it.

Consequently, he stumbled into the storage closet of metaphors and returned with an armload of word pictures. Did you notice how often John used the word *like?* He describes hair like wool, eyes like fire, feet like bronze, a voice like the noise of flooding water, and then says Jesus looked like the sun shining at its brightest time. The implication is clear. The human tongue is inadequate to describe Christ. So in a breathless effort to tell us what he saw, John gives us symbols. Symbols originally intended for and understood by members of seven churches in Asia.

For us to comprehend the passage we must understand the symbols as the original readers understood them.

By the way, John's strategy is not strange. We do the same. If you open your newspaper to an editorial page and see a donkey talking to an elephant, you know the meaning. This isn't a cartoon about a zoo; it is a cartoon about politics. (On second thought, maybe it is a cartoon about a zoo!) But you know the symbolism behind the images. And in order for us to understand John's vision, we must do the same. And as we do, as we begin to interpret the pictures, we gain glimpses of what we will see when we see Christ. Let's give it a go.

When we see Christ, what will we see?

We will see the perfect priest. "He was dressed in a long robe and had a gold band around his chest" (v. 13). The first readers of this message knew the significance of the robe and band. Jesus is wearing the clothing of a priest. A priest presents people to God and God to people.

You have known other priests. There have been others in your life, whether clergy or not, who sought to bring you to God. But they, too, needed a priest. Some needed a priest more than you did. They, like you, were sinful. Not so with Jesus. "Jesus is the kind of high priest we need. He is holy, sinless, pure, not influenced by sinners, and he is raised above the heavens" (Heb. 7:26).

Jesus is the perfect priest.

He is also pure and purifying: "His head and hair were white like wool, as white as snow, and his eyes were like flames of fire" (Rev. 1:14).

What would a person look like if he had never sinned? If no worry wrinkled his brow and no anger shadowed his eyes? If no bitterness snarled his lips and no selfishness bowed his smile? If a person had never sinned, how would he appear? We'll know when we see Jesus. What John saw that Sunday on Patmos was absolutely spotless. He was reminded of the virgin wool of sheep and the untouched snow of winter.

And John was also reminded of fire. Others saw the burning bush, the burning altar, the fiery furnace, or the fiery chariots, but John saw the fiery eyes. And in those eyes he saw a purging blaze that will burn the bacteria of sin and purify the soul.

A priest; white-haired, snow-pure, and white-hot. (Already we see this is no pale Galilean.) The image continues.

When we see Jesus we will see absolute strength. "His feet were like bronze that glows hot in a furnace" (v. 15).

John's audience knew the value of this metal. Eugene Peterson helps those of us who don't by explaining:

> Bronze is a combination of iron and copper. Iron is strong but it rusts. Copper won't rust but it's pliable. Combine the two in bronze and the best quality of each is preserved, the strength of the iron and the endurance of the copper. The rule of Christ is set on this base: the foundation of his power is tested by fire.[2]

Every power you have ever seen has decayed. The muscle men in the magazines, the automobiles on the racetrack, the armies in the history books. They had their strength and they had their day, but their day passed. But the strength of Jesus will never be surpassed. Never. When you see him, you will, for the first time, see true strength.

Up until this point, John has described what he saw. Now he tells what he heard. He shares the sound of Christ's voice. Not the words, but the sound, the tone, the timbre. The sound of a voice can be more important than the words of a voice. I can say, "I love you," but if I do so with a coerced grumble, you will not feel loved.

Ever wonder how you would feel if Jesus spoke to you? John felt like he was near a waterfall: "His voice was like the noise of flooding water" (v. 15).

The sound of a river rushing through a forest is not a timid one. It is the backdrop against all other sounds. Even when nature sleeps, the river speaks. The same is true of Christ. In heaven his voice is always heard—a steady, soothing, commanding presence.

In his hands are the seven stars. "He held seven stars in his right hand" (v. 16). We later read that "the seven stars are the angels of the seven churches" (v. 20). With apologies to southpaws, the right hand in Scripture is the picture of readiness. Joseph was blessed with Jacob's right hand (Gen. 48:18), the Red Sea was divided when God stretched out his right hand (Ex. 15:12), the right hand of God sustains us (Ps. 18:35), and Jesus is at the right hand of God interceding (Rom. 8:34). The right hand is a picture of action. And what does John see in the right hand of Christ? The angels of the churches. Like a soldier readies his sword or a carpenter grips his hammer, Jesus secures the angels, ready to send them to protect his people.

How welcome is this reassurance! How good to know that the pure, fiery, bronzed-footed Son of Man has one priority: the protection of his church. He holds them in the palm of his right hand. And he directs them with the sword of his word: "And a sharp double-edged sword came out of his mouth" (Rev. 1:16).

The sound of his voice soothes the soul, but the truth of his voice pierces the soul. "God's word is alive and working and is sharper than a double-edged sword. It cuts all the way into us, where the soul and spirit are joined, to the center of our joints and bones. And it judges the thoughts and feelings in our hearts. Nothing in all the world can be hidden from God" (Heb. 4:12–13).

No more charades. No more games. No more half-truths. Heaven is an honest land. It is a land where the shadows are banished by the face of Christ. "His face was like the sun shining in all its brilliance" (Rev. 1:16 NIV).

What are we to do with such a picture? How are we to assimilate these images? Are we to combine them on a canvas and consider it a portrait of Jesus? I don't think so. I don't think the goal of this vision is to tell us what Jesus looks like, but rather who Jesus is:

The Perfect Priest.
The Only Pure One.
The Source of Strength.
The Sound of Love.
The Everlasting Light.

And what will happen when you see Jesus?

You will see unblemished purity and unbending strength. You will feel his unending presence and know his unbridled protection. And—all that he is, you will be, for you will be like Jesus. Wasn't that the promise of John? "We know that when Christ comes again, we will be like him, because we will see him as he really is" (1 John 3:2).

Since you'll be pure as snow, you will never sin again.

Since you will be as strong as bronze, you will never stumble again.

Since you'll dwell near the river, you will never feel lonely again.

Since the work of the priest will have been finished, you will never doubt again.

When Christ comes, you will dwell in the light of God. And you will see him as he really is.

Thirteen

Crossing the Threshold

A Day of Everlasting Celebration

I promised to give you to Christ, as your only husband. I want to give you as his pure bride.

THE STORY OF THE PRINCE AND HIS PEASANT BRIDE. A more intriguing romance never occurred. His attraction to her is baffling. He, the stately prince. She, the common peasant. He, peerless. She, plain. Not ugly, but she can be. And often is. She tends to be sullen and sour, even cranky. Not the kind of soul you'd want to live with.

But according to the prince, she is the soul he can't live without. So he proposed to her. On the dusty floor of her peasant's cottage, he knelt, took her hand, and asked her to be his bride. Even the angels inclined an ear to hear her whisper, "Yes."

"I'll return for you soon," he promised.

"I will be waiting," she pledged.

No one thought it odd that the prince would leave. He is, after all, the son of the king. Surely he has some kingdom work to do. What's odd is not his departure, but her behavior during his absence. She forgets she's engaged!

You'd think the wedding would be ever on her mind, but it isn't. You'd think the day would be on the tip of her tongue. But it's not. Some of her friends have never heard her speak of the event. Days pass—even weeks—and his return isn't mentioned. Why, there have been times, perish the thought, when she has been seen cavorting with the village men. Flirting. Whispering. In the bright of day. Dare we wonder about her activities in the dark of night?

Is she rebellious? Maybe. But mostly, she is just forgetful. She keeps forgetting that she is engaged. That's no excuse, you say. Why, his return should be her every thought! How could a peasant forget her prince? How could a bride forget her groom?

That's a good question. How could we? You see, the story of the prince and his peasant bride is not an ancient fable. It's not a tale about them, but rather a portrayal of us. Are we not the bride of Christ? Have we not been set apart "as a pure bride to one husband" (2 Cor. 11:2 NLT)? Did God not say to us, "I will make you my promised bride forever" (Hos. 2:19 NCV)?

We are engaged to our maker! We, the peasants, have heard the promise of the prince. He entered our village, took our hand, and stole our hearts. Why, even the angels inclined their ears to hear us say, "Yes."

And the same angels must be puzzled at our behavior. We don't always act like we are engaged, do we? Days will pass—even weeks—and we'll say nothing about our wedding. Why, some of those who know us well don't even know our prince is coming. What's wrong? Are we rebellious? To a degree, but I think mostly we are just forgetful. Amnesic.

I stopped in a vitamin store last week. I asked a clerk to show me around. We passed a bottle on the shelf that looked familiar, a bottle of ginkgo. Just the week earlier my mom had told me she was taking ginkgo for her memory. I knew I had heard of the vitamin, but couldn't place where. Guess what I asked the clerk? I pointed to the bottle and said, "Help me remember what this is for." (He gave me a discount.)

To forget the purpose of ginkgo is one thing. But to forget our engagement to Christ is another. We need a reminder! May I offer an incentive?

You have captured God's heart.

I first witnessed the power of a marriage proposal in college. I shared a class with a girl who got engaged. I don't remember much about the class, except that the hour was early and the teacher was dull. (Doctors used to send insomniacs to his class for treatment.) I don't even remember the name of the girl. I do remember that she was shy and unsure of herself. She didn't stand out in the crowd and seemed to like it that way. No makeup. No dress-up. She was ordinary.

One day, however, that all began to change. Her hair changed.

Her dress changed. Even her voice changed. She spoke. She spoke with confidence. What made the difference?

Simple. She was chosen. A young man she loved looked her squarely in the eye and said, "Come and spend forever with me." And she was changed. Empowered by his proposal. Validated by his love. His love for her convinced her that she was worth loving.

God's love can do the same for us. We, like the girl, feel so common. Insecurities stalk us. Self-doubt plagues us. But the marriage proposal of the prince can change all that.

Want a cure for insecurity? An elixir for self-doubt? Then meditate on these words intended for you:

> My sister, my bride, you have thrilled my heart; you have thrilled my heart with a glance of your eyes, with one sparkle from your necklace. Your love is so sweet, my sister, my bride. Your love is better than wine, and your perfume smells better than any spice. . . . My sister, my bride, you are like a garden locked up, like a walled-in spring, a closed-up fountain. (Song 4:9–12)

Does such language strike you as strange? Do you find it odd to think of God as an enthralled lover? Do you feel awkward thinking of Jesus as a suitor intoxicated on love? If so, how else do you explain his actions? Did logic put God in a manger? Did common sense nail him to a cross? Did Jesus come to earth guided by a natural law of science? No, he came as a prince with his eye on the maiden, ready to battle even the dragon itself if that's what it took to win her hand.

And that is exactly what it took. It took a battle with the dragon of hell. He has "loved you with an everlasting love; [he has] drawn you with loving-kindness" (Jer. 31:3 NIV).

While writing this chapter, I received a phone call from a man wanting advice regarding his girlfriend. He didn't know what to do. Their work had them in different cities and their view of the relationship had them on two different pages. He was ready to get married; she was ready to give it some time. You should have heard the emotion in his voice. "I guess I can live without her," he said. "But I don't want to."

There is no doubt that Jesus can live without us, but he doesn't want to. He longs for his bride.

Have you ever noticed the way a groom looks at his bride during the wedding? I have. Perhaps it's my vantage point. As the minister of the wedding, I'm positioned next to the groom. Side by side we stand, he about to enter the marriage, I about to perform it. By the time we reach the altar, I've been with him for some time backstage as he tugged his collar and mopped his brow. His buddies reminded him that it's not too late to escape, and there's always a half-serious look in his eyes that he might. As the minister, I'm the one to give him the signal when it's our turn to step out of the wings up to the altar. He follows me into the chapel like a criminal walking to the gallows. But all that changes when she appears. And the look on his face is my favorite scene in the wedding.

Most miss it. Most miss it because they are looking at her. But when other eyes are on the bride, I sneak a peek at the groom. If the light is just so and the angle just right, I can see a tiny reflection in his eyes. Her reflection. And the sight of her reminds him why he is here. His jaw relaxes and his forced smile softens. He forgets he's wearing a tux. He forgets his sweat-soaked shirt. He forgets the bet he made that he wouldn't puke. When he sees her, any thought of escape becomes a joke again. For it's written all over his face, "Who could bear to live without this bride?"

And such are precisely the feelings of Jesus. Look long enough into the eyes of our Savior and, there, too, you will see a bride. Dressed in fine linen. Clothed in pure grace. From the wreath in her hair to the clouds at her feet, she is royal; she is the princess. She is the bride. His bride. Walking toward him, she is not yet with him. But he sees her, he awaits her, he longs for her.

"Who could bear to live without her?" you hear him whisper.

And who is that bride? Who is this beauty who occupies the heart of Jesus?

It is not nature. He loves his creation and creation groans to be with him, but he never called creation his bride.

It is not his angels. His angels are ever present to worship and serve him, but he never called the heavenly beings his bride.

Then who? Who is this bride about whom Jesus speaks and for whom Jesus longs? Who is this maiden who has captured the heart of God's Son?

You are. You have captured the heart of God. "As a man rejoices over his new wife, so your God will rejoice over you" (Isa. 62:5).

The challenge is to remember that. To meditate on it. To focus on it. To allow his love to change the way you look at you.

Do you ever feel unnoticed? New clothes and styles may help for a while. But if you want permanent change, learn to see yourself as God sees you: "He has covered me with clothes of salvation and wrapped me with a coat of goodness, like a bridegroom dressed for his wedding, like a bride dressed in jewels" (Isa. 61:10).

Does your self-esteem ever sag? When it does, remember what you are worth. "You were bought, not with something that ruins like gold or silver, but with the precious blood of Christ, who was like a pure and perfect lamb" (1 Peter 1:18–19).

Are you concerned whether the love will last? You needn't be. "It is not our love for God; it is God's love for us in sending his Son to be the way to take away our sins" (1 John 4:10).

Ever feel like you have nothing?

Just look at the gifts he has given you: He has sent his angels to care for you, his Holy Spirit to dwell in you, his church to encourage you, and his Word to guide you. You have privileges only a fiancée could have. Anytime you speak, he listens; make a request and he responds. He will never let you be tempted too much or stumble too far. Let a tear appear on your cheek, and he is there to wipe it. Let a love sonnet appear on your lips, and he is there to hear it. As much as you want to see him, he wants to see you more.

He is building a house for you. And with every swing of the hammer and cut of the saw, he's dreaming of the day he carries you over the threshold. "There are many rooms in my Father's house; I would not tell you this if it were not true. I am going there to prepare a place for you. After I go and prepare a place for you, I will come back and take you to be with me so that you may be where I am" (John 14:2–3).

You have been chosen by Christ. You are released from your old life in your old house, and he has claimed you as his beloved. "Then where is he?" you might ask. "Why hasn't he come?"

There is only one answer. His bride is not ready. She is still being prepared.

Engaged people are obsessed with preparation. The right dress. The right weight. The right hair and the right tux. They want everything to be right. Why? So their fiancée will marry them? No. Just the opposite. They want to look their best *because* their fiancée is marrying them.

The same is true for us. We want to look our best for Christ. We want our hearts to be pure and our thoughts to be clean. We want our faces to shine with grace and our eyes to sparkle with love. We want to be prepared.

Why? In hopes that he will love us? No. Just the opposite. Because he already does.

You are spoken for. You are engaged, set apart, called out, a holy bride. Forbidden waters hold nothing for you. You have been chosen for his castle. Don't settle for one-night stands in the arms of a stranger.

Be obsessed with your wedding date. Guard against forgetfulness. Be intolerant of memory lapses. Write yourself notes.

Memorize verses. Do whatever you need to do to remember. "Aim at what is in heaven. . . . Think only about the things in heaven" (Col. 3:1–2). You are engaged to royalty, and your Prince is coming to take you home.

With an Ear for
the Trumpet

When it comes to animals, our house is a zoo. I wonder if other folks have the strange experiences we do. We had a bird enter through the chimney and get stuck in the bedroom. Another one knocked himself silly flying into a window. We forgot to feed a goldfish for a week—and he survived. We let a rabbit nibble on a backyard plant—and he didn't. It seems we have more than our share of animal episodes. In fact, sometimes I wonder if God sends them our way so that I will have ample illustrations.

Such was my thought last week with Fred. Fred is one of the two hamsters under the domain of our nine-year-old daughter, Sara. She was letting him run up and down the piano keyboard. I don't know what Denalyn would have thought about a hamster on her new piano, but she wasn't home. Besides, I was presiding over the affair in fine fatherly fashion, stretched out on the couch. The little fellow wasn't doing any harm—he seemed to be having fun. I know we were. Sara and I got a good giggle out of Fred's wind sprints. He brought new meaning to "tickling the ivories." But after several dashes, all three of us were a bit tired. So Sara set Fred where you place the sheet music. I closed my eyes and Sara, for just a moment, stepped away from the piano. Just a moment was all Fred needed to get into trouble.

To understand what happened next, you need to know that our piano is one of the horizontal versions. Had the piano been of the upright sort, Fred would have been safe. Had the lid been closed, Fred would have been safe. But the lid was open and Sara was distracted and I was dozing off when Fred decided to peer over the edge.

I opened my eyes just in time to see him tumble into a pool of piano strings and hammers. Sara and I both sprang into action, but it was too late. Our little friend was not only inside the instrument, he was under the strings. We could see his furry back rubbing against the wires as he ran back and forth looking for a way to escape.

Fred was trapped.

And we were stumped. How do you get a hamster out of a piano? We tried several approaches.

We tried nudging him. Wedging our fingers between the wires, we tried to coax him toward the opening. Didn't work.

He ran the opposite direction and disappeared in a corner. We couldn't see him. We held a lamp over the piano and still couldn't see him. We tried flashlights and still couldn't see him. Coaxing didn't work.

So we tried calling him out of hiding. We used every voice possible.

The voice of a search party: "Fred, can you hear us?"

The voice of a friend: "Come on Fred, old buddy."

The voice of a mother: "Freddie-pooh, where are you?"

Even the voice of a drill sergeant: "Fred. Get out!"

Nothing worked. Coaxing didn't work. Calling didn't work. So we came up with another idea. How about a little piano music? We had to be careful; certain songs could be dangerous. A rousing rendition of John Philip Sousa might knock him out. So we were delicate, softly touching first this key, then that, then pausing to listen for the sound of little feet. We heard nothing. We played more and listened more. Still no luck. We tried some creative tunes. We thought "Three Blind Mice" might make him homesick. "I've Got You Under My Strings" seemed appropriate. We even attempted a variation of "Pop, Goes the Hamster." But he didn't get the message. He refused to come out of his hiding place.

Only one alternative remained. We had to *(gulp!)* dismantle the piano. Some of you would not be intimidated by this task. I was. My hands are anything but handy. I have trouble opening a loaf of bread, much less opening a musical instrument. But Fred, the hamster, was in danger. Could we bear the thought of him stranded in the piano? Could we bear the smell of him stranded in the piano? So I grabbed my trusty Phillips screwdriver and began looking for a place to start.

I couldn't find one. The frame had no bolts. The keyboard had no screws. I figured out how to remove a pedal, but that wasn't much help.

So, once again, we were trapped. All of us were trapped. Fred hadn't come up for air, and we hadn't come up with a solution. All we could do was pray that he survive the night and call a piano tuner in the morning. I hadn't quite figured out what to say to the tuner, however. ("No, the piano sounds fine. But we have a hamster who really gets into his music.")

It was when we sat down to take a break that I wondered, *Do these things happen to other families? Or does God know that I need a conclusion for the book?*

If so, he certainly gave me a good one with Fred. We have a lot in common—you and I do—with Sara's pet. Like Fred, we took a fall. And, like Fred, we are trapped. Trapped, not by piano wires, but by guilt, anxiety, and pride. This is a foreign, fearful place. We were never meant to be here. Somehow we know, we were never meant to be this far from our Master's hand. We don't know how to get out.

But God does. He is not baffled. And he wants us to know that he will soon come and take us home. Isn't this the final declaration of the Bible? "I'm on my way! I'll be there soon!" (Rev. 22:20 MSG). But do we pay attention? Some do. But others of us, like

Fred, are a bit slow to respond. Thankfully, God understands. And he gets creative.

He coaxes. Through the fingers of circumstance and situation, he tries to get us to look up. But we, like Fred, make a dash for the corner.

He calls for us. Sometimes whispering. Other times shouting. But we don't always answer.

So he provides some music. Divine fingers touch the keyboard of the universe. We are treated to regular symphonies of sunrises and sunsets. Soaring eagles and slapping waves. All intended to get our attention. But most stay in the corners.

God has even been known to do a little dismantling. Those times when our world seems to be falling apart? God's been known to pull out a Phillips and shake things up a bit—not because he doesn't love us. Just the opposite. He loves us dearly. And he will do whatever it takes to rescue his children.

Even if it means becoming one of us and entering our world.

I said it jokingly to the girls. After we had tried everything possible, I said, "Well, if one of us could become a hamster, we could go in and show Fred the way out."

Of course we couldn't even begin to do such a thing. But can you imagine if you could? Can you imagine becoming like Fred? Taking on a round belly, short legs, and whiskers? (Some of you think I just described your husband.) Leaving your great world for his cramped world? Why, we couldn't imagine such an act. But God could—and God did. And the journey from human to hamster is nothing compared to the span between heaven and earth. God became a baby. He entered a world, not of piano strings and hammers, but a world of problems and heartaches.

"The Word became human and lived here on earth among us. He was full of unfailing love and faithfulness" (John 1:14 NLT).

The operative word of the verse is *among*. He lived *among* us. He donned the costliest of robes: a human body. He made a throne out of a manger and a royal court out of some cows. He took a common name—Jesus—and made it holy. He took common people and made them the same. He could have lived over us or away from us. But he didn't. He lived *among* us.

He became a friend of the sinner and brother of the poor. He touched their sores and felt their tears and paid for their mistakes. He entered a tomb and came out and pledged that we'd do the same. And to us all, and to all the frightened Freds of the world, he shared the same message. "Don't let your hearts be troubled. Trust in God, and trust in me. . . . I will come back and take you to be with me so that you may be where I am" (John 14:1, 3).

And how do we respond?

Some pretend he doesn't exist. They occupy themselves with a study of the piano and ask no questions about the Maestro.

Others hear him, but don't believe him. It's not easy to believe that God would go so far to take us home.

But then, a few decide to give it a try. They venture out of their corners and peek up through the opening. Each day they look toward the sky. They, like Simeon, "wait for" and "look forward to" the day Christ comes (2 Peter 3:12). They know there is more to life than the belly of a piano, and they want to be ready when Christ comes.

Be numbered among the searchers, won't you? Live with an ear for the trumpet and an eye for the clouds. And when he calls your name, be ready.

Oh, you might wonder whatever happened to Fred. Well, he finally made his way back to the place where he fell in. He looked up. And when he did, Sara was there. He lifted his head just high enough so that she could reach in and lift him out.

Which is exactly what God will do for you. You will look up, and he will reach down and take you home . . .

when Christ comes.

NOTES

CHAPTER 1: "YOU DO THE TRUSTING; I'LL DO THE TAKING"

1. John MacArthur, *The Glory of Heaven* (Wheaton, IL: Crossway Books, 1996), 118.
2. *Titanic Live*, broadcast on the Discovery Channel, 16 August 1998; *PrimeTime Live*, 13 August 1998.

CHAPTER 3: THE CRADLE OF HOPE

1. Jack Canfield and Mark Hansen, *Chicken Soup for the Soul* (Deerfield Beach, FL: Health Communications, 1993), 273–74.
2. John R. W. Stott, *Basic Christianity* (Downers Grove, IL: InterVarsity, 1971), 50.

CHAPTER 4: INTO THE WARM ARMS OF GOD

1. Taken from Bob Russell, *Favorite Stories* (Louisville, KY: The Living Word Ministries), audiotape.

2. Anthony Hoekema, *The Bible and the Future* (Grand Rapids, MI: Eerdmans, 1979), 104. *Analysai* (to depart) is an aorist infinitive, depicting the momentary experience of death. Linked to *analysai* by a single article is the present infinitive, *einai* (to be). The single article ties the two infinitives together so that the actions depicted by the infinitives are two aspects of the same thing, like two sides of the same coin. Paul is saying here that the moment he departs or dies, that very moment, he will be with Christ.

CHAPTER 5: THE BRAND-NEW YOU

1. Unless, of course, you are alive when Christ returns, and then you will also get a new body. Paul says this in 1 Corinthians 15:51.
2. Hans-Joachim Kraus, *Charisma der Theologie,* as quoted in John Piper, *Future Grace* (Sisters, OR: Multnomah Books, 1995), 370.
3. Joni Eareckson Tada, *Heaven: Your Real Home* (Grand Rapids, MI: Zondervan, 1995), 39.
4. Luke 24:13–35; John 20:10–18; John 21:12–14.
5. John 20:14; John 21:1–4; Luke 24:16; John 20:26.

CHAPTER 6: A NEW WARDROBE

1. David Danner, "Rock of Ages."
2. Edward Mote, "The Solid Rock."

CHAPTER 9: THE LAST DAY OF EVIL

1. I wrote about this more fully in *The Great House of God.* For a more in-depth treatment of this truth, see pages 143–55.
2. Joe Beam, *Seeing the Unseen* (West Monroe, LA: Howard, 1994), 230.

CHAPTER 10: ITEMIZED GRACE

1. J. C. Ryle as quoted by John Blanchard in *Whatever Happened to Hell?* (Wheaton, IL: Crossway Books, 1995), 184.

2. Donald Bloesch, *Essentials of Evangelical Theology* (San Francisco: Harper and Row, 1978), 229.

Chapter 11: Love's Caution

1. C. S. Lewis, as quoted in Larry Dixon, *The Other Side of the Good News* (Wheaton, IL: Victor Books, 1992), 45.
2. For two contrasting views on the duration of hell, consider Blanchard, *Whatever Happened to Hell?* and Edward William Fudge, *The Fire That Consumes* (Carlisle, UK: The Paternoster Press, 1994).
3. Blanchard, *Whatever Happened to Hell?*, 130.
4. C. S. Lewis, *The Great Divorce* (New York: Macmillan, 1946), 66–67. As quoted in Blanchard, *Whatever Happened to Hell?*, 151.
5. C. S. Lewis, *The Problem of Pain* (New York: Macmillan, 1967), 127. As quoted in Blanchard, *Whatever Happened to Hell?*, 152.

Chapter 12: Seeing Jesus

1. Peter Kreeft, *Heaven: The Heart's Deepest Longing* (San Francisco: Ignatius Press, 1980), 49.
2. Eugene Peterson, *Reversed Thunder* (San Francisco: HarperSanFrancisco, 1988), 36–37.

WHEN CHRIST COMES

Study Guide

As Prepared by Steve Halliday

WHEN CHRIST COMES

LOOKING BACK

1. How do you respond to Max's description of Christ's return? How do you think you'd respond if you really saw the return of Christ?

2. What one word would you use to summarize your emotions regarding the return of Christ? Discomfort? Denial? Disappointment? Obsession? Joy?

3. What do you think Max meant when he wrote, "Some of you were only a few lines into the opening description of the return before you stubbed an opinion on a sentence"? Did *you* "stub an opinion"? If so, explain.

LOOKING AHEAD

1. Read John 14:1–3. What was Jesus' main purpose in telling us about his return?
2. Read Matthew 24:30–31. How does Jesus picture his return?

LOOKING IN

1. When was the last time you pondered the Lord's return? How did your thoughts affect the rest of your day?
2. As you're reading *When Christ Comes*, determine to do your own biblical study on Christ's return, especially focusing on the present-day effects of such a study.

ONE

"YOU DO THE TRUSTING; I'LL DO THE TAKING"

LOOKING BACK

1. "We don't want our kids to sweat the details."
   A. Why don't we want our kids to sweat the details? What can happen when they *do* sweat the details?
   B. How does this idea apply to our relationship with God?

2. "'You do the trusting and I'll do the taking.' A healthy reminder when it comes to anticipating the return of Christ. For many, the verb *trust* is not easily associated with his coming."

    A. What does Max mean by "You do the trusting and I'll do the taking"?

    B. Why do so many people have trouble connecting "trust" with Christ's coming? Do *you* have such trouble? Explain.

3. "Don't be troubled by the return of Christ. Don't be anxious about things you cannot comprehend. Issues like the millennium and the Antichrist are intended to challenge and stretch us, but not overwhelm and certainly not divide us. For the Christian, the return of Christ is not a riddle to be solved or a code to be broken, but rather a day to be anticipated."

    A. How can an issue that we can't fully comprehend still "challenge and stretch us"?

    B. How can such issues "overwhelm" or "divide" us?

    C. How can we make sure that such issues don't overwhelm or divide us?

4. Max outlines three truths that Jesus gave to keep us from being troubled:

    • "I have ample space for you."
    • "I have a prepared place for you."
    • "I'm not kidding."

    A. What's important about each of these three truths? How can they help to keep us from being troubled?

B. Which of these truths is most significant to you personally? Why?

LOOKING AHEAD

1. Read John 14:1–3.

   A. On a day-by-day basis, how do you "trust in God"? What does this trust look like for you?

   B. What is the primary reason for Christ's return, according to verse 3?

2. Read 1 Thessalonians 1:9–10.

   A. What specific actions did the Thessalonians take once they came to Christ? How do they provide a pattern for us?

   B. How do you actively wait for Christ to return?

3. Read Hebrews 10:23–25.

   A. "The day" the writer mentions in verse 25 is the day Christ returns to earth. How does he say we are to act until then? How is our behavior related to Christ's return, in the writer's view?

LOOKING IN

1. Do you find it easy or hard to trust God with the details of your life? Explain.

2. Determine this week to have a significant conversation with a fellow believer about the return of Christ. How can you encourage each other in your walk of faith by discussing Christ's return?

Two

Waiting Forwardly

Looking Back

1. Max writes that Scripture characterizes Abraham as *trusting*, Moses as *leading*, Paul as *writing*, John as *loving*, and Simeon as *looking*.

   A. For the Christian, how are these traits significant?

   B. How do you think Scripture would characterize you?

2. "Simeon is a man on tiptoe, wide-eyed and watching for the one who will come to save Israel."

   A. Do you see this as a picture of active or passive looking? Explain.

   B. How would you describe your own waiting for the coming of Christ?

3. "The master loves to find people looking for his return. The master rewards those who 'wait forwardly.'"

   A. What does it mean to "wait forwardly"?

   B. Why do you think the master loves to find people anticipating his return?

4. "Hope of the future is not a license for irresponsibility in the present."

   A. What does Max mean by this statement?

   B. From your own experience, describe how someone's

hope of the future prompted them to act irresponsibly in the present. What happened? How could it have been avoided?

LOOKING AHEAD

1. Read 2 Peter 3:11–12 NIV.

   A. According to Peter, how should our hope of the future affect our lives? Is this principle at work in your own life? Explain.

   B. Peter says we can "speed" the coming of "the day of God." How?

2. Read Luke 2:25–35.

   A. What did Simeon say about Jesus in verses 29–32?

   B. How did Jesus' parents react to this in verse 33? Why?

   C. What did Simeon tell Mary about Jesus in verses 34–35? What events are predicted here?

3. Read Matthew 24:36–44.

   A. What is the primary admonition given to us in these verses? What are we to do now? How do we do this?

   B. What do these verses say about setting a date or time for Christ's return? How should we react when people do this? Explain.

LOOKING IN

1. All of us have times during the week when we find ourselves waiting—in line at the checkout stand, in the

mechanic's shop, in a doctor's office. Determine this week to use some of this "waiting time" to meditate on "waiting forwardly" for the return of Jesus. Then at the end of the week, tell someone about your experience. How has it affected the way you live?

2. Try to put yourself in Simeon's place. How has it felt to wait all those years for the Messiah? How has your waiting changed the way you live? How did it feel when you finally saw the Savior? How will you live from that time on? Now shift forward to the present again. How can you adopt some of the strategies pioneered by Simeon? What might happen if you did?

THREE

THE CRADLE OF HOPE

LOOKING BACK

1. "No matter what happens, I'll always be there for you."

A. Why did the son in this story believe his father's promise? What difference did it make to the son that he had this promise?

B. Does God give us such a promise? Explain.

2. "Yes, the rocks will tumble. Yes, the ground will shake. But the child of God needn't fear—for the Father has promised to take us to be with him."

A. How does such a promise give us practical help when the rocks tumble and the ground shakes?

B. Describe a time in your life when the rocks tumbled and the ground shook—but the promise of Christ's return buoyed up your soul.

3. "For Paul and any follower of Christ, the promise is simply this: The resurrection of Jesus is proof and preview of our own."

A. How is the resurrection of Christ "proof and preview" of our own resurrection?

B. How can this give us comfort in difficult times?

4. "In the blink of an eye, as fast as the lightning flashes from the east to the west, he will come back. And everyone will see him—you will, I will. Bodies will push back the dirt and break the surface of the sea. The earth will tremble, the sky will roar, and those who do not know him will shudder. But in that hour you will not fear, because you know him."

A. How would you feel if Christ were to come back this instant? Explain.

B. Max says those who don't know Christ at his return will "shudder," while those who know him "will not fear." Why the difference?

5. Max mentions three alternatives to the idea that Christ rose from the grave:

- Jesus never actually died; he simply fainted on the cross.
- Jesus' disciples stole his body from the tomb.
- The Jews stole Jesus' body from the tomb.

A. How would you respond to each of these alternative theories? What problems does each have?

LOOKING AHEAD

1. Read 1 Corinthians 15:22–23.

    A. What two groups of people are described in this passage? To which group do you belong? How do you know?

    B. Why does this passage depend on the truth of 1 Corinthians 15:17? What's the connection?

2. Read Romans 6:5–9.

    A. What connection does the apostle Paul make between Christ's death and resurrection and our own?

    B. How should this truth affect us in the here-and-now, according to Paul?

3. Read 1 Thessalonians 4:14.

    A. What promise is given here? How is this promise designed to give us hope?

LOOKING IN

1. After preparing yourself in prayer, determine this week to speak about Jesus' resurrection to someone who doesn't yet

know Christ. What hope does his resurrection bring you?
How can your friend benefit from this same hope?

2. Have a discussion this week with your children or other
members of your family about the significance of the
resurrection for daily living. How does it affect your life?

Four

Into the Warm Arms of God

Looking Back

1. "Can you remember the first time death forced you to say
good-bye?"

    A. Answer Max's question. Describe this time.

    B. Describe the most recent time death forced you to say
    good-bye. How was this different from the first time?

2. "Just as a parent needs to know that his or her child is safe at
school, we long to know that our loved ones are safe in death."

    A. Do you agree with Max? Why or why not?

    B. How can loved ones be "safe in death"? What does this
    mean?

3. "When speaking about the period between the death of the
body and the resurrection of the body, the Bible doesn't
shout; it just whispers."

A. Why do you think the Bible merely "whispers" about this period?

B. What's the best way to react to this whisper?

4. "'What Paul is saying here is that the moment he departs or dies, that very moment he is with the Christ.'"

A. How can this truth give hope to terminally ill individuals?

B. How can this truth give hope to those loved ones who are left behind?

LOOKING AHEAD

1. Read 1 Thessalonians 4:13–18 NIV.

A. According to verse 13, how do "the rest of men" grieve when they lose a loved one? Why do they grieve in this way?

B. Who is coming back with Jesus, according to Paul?

C. Which is the one group that will never taste death, according to verse 17?

2. Read Philippians 1:21–26 NIV.

A. What was Paul's internal struggle in this passage? How was he "torn"?

B. What did Paul expect would happen the moment he died? Explain.

3. Read Acts 7:54–60 NIV.

A. What did Stephen see before he died? Why did this fill him with hope? Why did it so anger the crowd?

B. What does it mean that Stephen "fell asleep"? Why use this terminology?

LOOKING IN

1. Try an experiment for one week. Attempt to engage several people in conversation about death and dying. What kind of reactions do you get?

2. Spend some time this week thinking about your own funeral. What aspects of this event would be celebratory? What would you want to be said? Who would you want to be there? Why?

FIVE

THE BRAND-NEW YOU

LOOKING BACK

1. "Out of the decay of the seed comes the birth of a plant."
   A. Why is this principle from agriculture important to spiritual faith?
   B. How does this principle look backward and forward at the same time?

2. "The graveside service is not a burial, but a planting. The grave is not a hole in the ground, but a fertile furrow. The cemetery is not the resting place, but rather the transformation place."

A. Explain what Max means by this statement.

B. Do you normally think like this? Why or why not?

3. Max says God will transform our bodies in three ways, from:

- Corruption to incorruption.
- Dishonor to glory.
- Weakness to power.

A. What is involved with each of these three ways? What is the significance of each?

B. How can we use this knowledge to transform the way we live now?

4. Max offers two complementary truths to end this chapter:

- Your body, in some form, will last forever. Respect it.
- Your pain will NOT last forever. Believe it.

A. How do you "respect" your body? How can you disrespect it?

B. How do we sometimes show that we have forgotten our pain will not last forever? How can we make sure that we won't forget this truth?

LOOKING AHEAD

1. Read 1 Corinthians 15:20–26 NIV.

A. In what way is Christ the "firstfruits" of those who have "fallen asleep"?

B. What is the last "enemy" to be destroyed?

2. Read 1 Corinthians 15:35–44.

  A. How does Paul say our bodies are like a seed? How does this analogy help to explain our future bodies?

  B. Name some of the differences between our present bodies and our future bodies.

3. Read Philippians 3:20–21.

  A. How will our bodies be transformed?

  B. What will our new bodies be like?

  C. Who will accomplish this?

4. Read John 20:10–21:14; Luke 24:36–43.

  A. How was Jesus' resurrection body like his mortal body?

  B. How was Jesus' resurrection body unlike his mortal body?

  C. What significance does this hold for us?

LOOKING IN

1. In a single sitting, read the accounts of Jesus' post-resurrection appearances found in each of the four Gospels. Try to put yourself in the disciples' place—how do you think you would have reacted to these appearances? What do you think these appearances did for the disciples' faith? What can they do for your own faith?

2. Spend some time daydreaming about the potential of your future glorified body. What about your present body will be better? What do you think it will be like to have such a strong,

amazing body? What do you imagine you will do with it? At the conclusion of your daydreaming, spend some more time thanking God that this new body he speaks of in Scripture isn't merely a daydream, but will surely come into being. In you!

SIX

A NEW WARDROBE

LOOKING BACK

1. "I had made it all the way to the door but was denied entrance."

   A. Why was Max denied entrance to the locker room at Augusta National Country Club?

   B. How do you think Max felt when he was denied entrance? How would you have felt?

2. "To be turned away from seeing golf history is one thing, but to be refused admission into heaven is quite another. That is why some people don't want to discuss the return of Christ. It makes them nervous. They may be God-fearing and church-attending but still nervous."

   A. Does discussing the return of Christ ever make you nervous? Explain.

   B. Do you ever worry that you will be refused entrance into heaven? Explain.

3. "God sees what you and I miss. For as Mr. Decent walks through life, he makes mistakes. And every time he sins, a stain appears on his clothing. For example, he stretched the truth when he spoke to his boss yesterday. He was stained. He fudged, ever so slightly, on his expense report. Another stain. The other guys were gossiping about the new employee and, rather than walk away, he chimed in. Still another. From our perspective, these aren't big deals. But our perspective doesn't matter. God's does. And what God sees is a man wrapped in mistakes."

   A. Is it easier to see other people's stains or our own? Explain.

   B. Do you think God sees a person "wrapped in mistakes" when he looks at you? Explain.

4. "He did more than remove our coat; he put on our coat. And he wore our coat of sin to the cross. As he died, his blood flowed over our sins. They were cleansed by his blood. And because of this, when Christ comes, we have no fear of being turned away at the door."

   A. What "coat" of ours did Christ put on? How was that "coat" made clean?

   B. What kind of "coat" are you wearing right now? How do you know?

LOOKING AHEAD

1. Read 1 John 2:28 NIV.

   A. To whom is this verse addressed? How is this significant?

B. How can we make sure we are "unashamed" at the coming of Christ?

2. Read Matthew 22:1–14.
   A. Why did the first group of invited guests (vs. 4–6) not come to the king's banquet?
   B. Describe the second group of guests who were invited to the king's banquet (vs. 9–10).
   C. What is the significance of the man who was found at the banquet without wedding clothes (vs. 11–13)? What is Jesus' point?

3. Read Romans 13:14 and Galatians 3:26–29.
   A. What sort of clothing is described here? What is its significance?
   B. How does one put on this sort of clothing? Have you put it on? Explain.

4. Read Galatians 3:13 and 2 Corinthians 5:21.
   A. In what way did Christ take our place?
   B. What was the purpose of this exchange?

LOOKING IN

1. Sometimes we think the best way to make sure we are "unashamed" at the coming of Christ is to focus on cutting out of our lives all the things that might make us ashamed— and therefore end up concentrating on our sin rather than on Christ. For a couple of days, try this experiment instead:

Consciously dwell on the idea that Christ could return at any moment. Think about him, not your sin—and then describe your experience in a personal journal.

2. Read a book that chronicles the ability of Jesus Christ to transform the lives of all kinds of people (like Max Lucado's *Just Like Jesus*). Then spend several minutes thanking God for what he is doing in your own life.

SEVEN

LOOK WHO'S IN THE WINNER'S CIRCLE!

LOOKING BACK

1. "We cheered because he did what we wanted to do. Wasn't there a time when you wanted to be where Mark McGwire was? Think a little. Scroll back a bit. Wasn't there a younger, more idealistic you who dreamed of hitting the big ball? Or winning the Pulitzer? Or singing on Broadway? Or commanding a fleet? Or receiving the Nobel Peace Prize? Or clutching an Oscar?"

   A. If you're a baseball fan, how did you react to McGwire's amazing season?

   B. If you're not particularly a baseball fan, what dream did you once nurture as a younger person? Describe that dream.

2. "Heavenly rewards are not limited to a chosen few, but 'to all those who have waited with love for him to come again'" (2 Tim. 4:8).

　A. Why do you think God tells us in advance about rewards? How often do you think of heavenly rewards? Explain.

　B. Do you think a heavenly reward is waiting for you? Explain.

3. Max mentions three types of crowns:

　• The crown of life.
　• The crown of righteousness.
　• The crown of glory.

　A. What is the significance of each of these crowns?

　B. Which of these crowns means the most to you? Why?

4. "Heaven will be wonderful, not only because of what is present, but because of what is absent."

　A. How can something be wonderful because of what it lacks?

　B. What kind of things will heaven lack? How does this make you feel?

Looking Ahead

1. Read Matthew 24:42–47 NIV.

　A. Why does Jesus compare his return to a break-in by a thief? How are the two alike? How are they different?

B. How do verses 42–44 define what a "faithful and wise" servant is?

C. How will the Lord reward "faithful and wise" servants (vs. 46–47)?

2. Read 2 Timothy 4:6–8.

A. Describe Paul's circumstances when he penned these words. How did the ideas he wrote about encourage his own heart?

B. What sort of crown is mentioned here? To whom is it given? Do you expect to receive this crown? Explain.

3. Read James 1:12.

A. Describe the person James has in view in this verse. Why is this significant?

B. What crown does James mention here? To whom is it given? Do you expect to receive this crown? Explain.

4. Read 1 Peter 5:1–4.

A. Describe the person Peter has in view in this verse.

B. What crown does Peter mention here? To whom is it given? Do you expect to receive this crown? Explain.

LOOKING IN

1. Take a few moments to envision yourself in heaven's "winner's circle." Imagine that all of heaven is focused on you. What is God saying about your life on earth? What sort of rewards do you think you might receive? Now shift back

to this moment in time. Do you need to make any changes in your life in order to receive the kind of rewards you'd like? If so, what? Ask God for the strength to do what you really believe you need to do and thank him for the rewards he's already described for us.

2. Get a concordance and look up the words *reward* and *inheritance*. Consider only those verses that talk about our eternal reward. What did you learn in your study that you didn't know before? What effect did your study have on the way you live today?

Eight

You'd Do It All Again

Looking Back

1. "Schindler saw the faces of the delivered; you will, too. Schindler heard the gratitude of the redeemed; you'll hear the same. He stood in a community of rescued souls; the same is reserved for you."

   A. Would it have been difficult to do what Schindler did? Explain.

   B. What is difficult about trying to live a godly life here on earth? Explain.

   C. How can focusing on others help us to keep moving forward in our spiritual walk?

2. "Most of us wonder what influence we have. (Which is good, for if we knew, we might grow arrogant.)"
   A. Do you ever wonder what influence you have? Explain.
   B. Why might we grow arrogant if we knew the whole story?

3. Max writes about "an awestruck joy which declares, 'I'm so proud of your faith.'"
   A. What will prompt this kind of awestruck joy? What part can you play in it?
   B. How is it possible to be "proud" of someone's faith? Isn't pride a sin?

4. Max says two things will happen in heaven if we find out how our faith has influenced that of others:

   • The grandeur and glory of the moment will far outstrip any description.
   • We won't regret any sacrifice we made for the kingdom.

   A. How can you maximize your influence for the kingdom?
   B. What kind of "sacrifices" is God calling you to make for the kingdom? How do you respond to these calls? Explain.

LOOKING AHEAD

1. Read 1 Thessalonians 2:17–20.
   A. What does Paul call the Christians in Thessalonica (v. 17)? How do you think he feels about them? Explain.
   B. What three things does Paul call the Christians in

Thessalonica in verse 19? How does Paul think he'll feel
about them when Christ returns?

2. Read 1 Corinthians 1:9.

   A. What does this verse tell us about the day Christ returns?

   B. Compare this verse to Isaiah 64:4. How has Paul slightly
   changed the verse in 1 Corinthians? What significance do
   you think this might have?

3. Read Acts 17:1–10.

   A. What do you learn about the birth of the church in
   Thessalonica?

   B. What clues do you get from this text about the difficulties
   the Thessalonians faced in their newfound faith? How can
   their experience help and encourage us today?

LOOKING IN

1. Sit down at a table, take a pad of paper and a pen or pencil,
   and try to list as many people as possible on whom you
   might have an influence. Family members? Friends? Church
   acquaintances? Store clerks? Gas station attendants? Paperboy?
   Neighbors? Then try to think about the last time you saw
   these people. What kind of influence did you probably have on
   them? Could you have influenced them toward Christ?

2. Spend a significant amount of time asking God to help you
   be the influence for him that you really want to be. Ask
   him to give you insight into ways to be a strong influence,

and ask him to show you what you might need to change
to become the most effective influence you can be. Then
thank him for hearing your prayer and allowing you to be an
influence in your world for him.

NINE

THE LAST DAY OF EVIL

LOOKING BACK

1. "If we aren't acquainted with the end of the script, we can grow
   fearful in the play. That's why it's wise to ponder the last act."
   A. What does Max mean by "the play"? How about "the end
   of the script"?
   B. How can we ponder "the last act"?

2. "God hasn't kept the ending a secret. He wants us to see the
   big picture. He wants us to know that he wins. And he also
   wants us to know that the evil we witness on the stage of life
   is not as mighty as we might think."
   A. Is Satan frightening to you?
   B. How does God "win" in the end? How do you encourage
   yourself to think about this ultimate divine victory?

3. Max gives us two reasons to be encouraged now despite
   whatever pain we might have to endure at the hands of evil:

- Jesus is praying for us.
- We will prevail.

A. Speculate for a moment: What kind of prayers do you think Jesus is offering on your behalf? Why these prayers?

B. In what way will we prevail? What will this look like? How does this make you feel? Explain.

LOOKING AHEAD

1. Read Revelation 20:10.

A. What is the ultimate destiny of the devil? How does this happen? Who ensures that it happens?

B. Why would the apostle John tell us about this event? How can it help us today?

2. Read Luke 22:31–34.

A. Why is it significant that Jesus said Satan "asked" to sift Peter as wheat?

B. What prayer did Jesus offer on Peter's behalf?

C. What confidence did Jesus have that his prayer would be answered?

D. Why is this conversation especially significant in light of what Jesus predicted in verse 34? How does verse 33 show that Peter's confidence was misplaced?

3. Read Hebrews 7:20–26 and Romans 8:26–27.

A. What promises are given to us in these two passages?

B. Why do you think we are given these promises? What is the point?

4. Read John 16:33.

A. What promise does Jesus give us about life in this world?

B. Why should we be encouraged even in difficult circumstances?

LOOKING IN

1. Memorize Hebrews 7:25–26 and Romans 8:26–27. Write these verses on cards and put them where you can see them when you go about your daily tasks. Thank God that he has not left you alone, that his eye is constantly on you, and that Jesus himself prays for you and your needs.

2. If you have children, think of a creative way to emphasize for them the truth that Jesus prays for them constantly. Create a little story or craft that will teach them about God's continual love and care for them. And make sure that you believe whatever you tell them!

TEN

ITEMIZED GRACE

LOOKING BACK

1. Max says the day of judgment at Christ's return will be marked by three accomplishments:

_____

- God's grace will be revealed.
- Rewards for God's servants will be unveiled.
- Those who do not know God will pay a price.

  A. How will God's grace be revealed at the second coming
     of Christ?
  B. How will God's rewards be unveiled?
  C. What kind of price will be paid by those who don't know
     God?

2. "What God did in Noah's generation, he will do at Christ's
   return. He will pronounce a universal, irreversible
   judgment. A judgment in which grace is revealed, rewards
   are unveiled, and the impenitent are punished."
   A. How will Christ's second coming be like what happened
      in Noah's day?
   B. How can we, like Noah, prepare for that day?

3. Max asks four "fundamental questions" about Christ's
   judgment:

   - Who will be judged?
   - What will be judged?
   - Why will Christians be judged?
   - What is the destiny of those who don't know Christ?

   A. What answer does Max give for each of these questions?
   B. What do you think of the answers Max gives? Do you
      think he's right? Explain.

4. "God's merciful verdict will echo through the universe. For the first time in history, we will understand the depth of his goodness. Itemized grace. Catalogued kindness. Registered forgiveness. We will stand in awe as one sin after another is proclaimed, and then pardoned."

    A. What does Max mean by "itemized grace"? How will this show God's goodness?

    B. Are you ready for the day of judgment? Explain.

LOOKING AHEAD

1. Read Genesis 6:5–14; 7:17–23.

    A. What do these passages teach us about God's response to sin?

    B. How do these passages prefigure what God will once again do in response to sin?

2. Read Matthew 24:31–46.

    A. What groups are judged as described in these passages?

    B. On what basis are they judged?

    C. What is the final outcome of this judgment for all groups concerned?

3. Read Romans 14:10–12.

    A. Which group is in view in these verses?

    B. On what basis are the members of this group judged?

4. Read 1 Corinthians 3:10–15.

    A. What kind of judgment will Christians undergo?

B. What are the possible results of this judgment? What is not possible?

5. Read 2 Thessalonians 1:6–10.

A. What is the destiny of those who don't know God?

B. In your opinion, what is the worst part of this destiny? Explain.

LOOKING IN

1. Compare 2 Timothy 2:19 with Titus 1:15–16. As you take inventory of your life, how can you increasingly demonstrate that you belong to Christ? How can you make sure that your life does not "deny" Christ? How can you help others to live the pure lives God intends for his people?

2. Over the course of a day, make a mental list of all the acts of grace God has shown to you in just the last year. Then at the end of the day, give thanks to God for each one of these graces he has brought to your mind.

ELEVEN

LOVE'S CAUTION

LOOKING BACK

1. Max quotes C. S. Lewis, who wrote: "There is no doctrine which I would more willingly remove from Christianity than

[hell], if it lay in my power. . . . I would pay any price to be able to say truthfully: 'All will be saved.'"

A. Do you resonate with Lewis's comment? Explain.

B. Why cannot we truthfully say, "All will be saved"?

2. "If there is no hell, God is not just. If there is no punishment of sin, heaven is apathetic toward the rapists and pillagers and mass murderers of society."

A. Why would God not be just if there were no hell?

B. How does punishment of sin show heaven is not apathetic toward wickedness?

3. "The New Testament is the primary storehouse of thoughts on hell. And Jesus is the primary teacher. No one spoke of eternal punishment more often or more clearly than Christ himself."

A. How are these facts significant? How do they make you feel? Why?

B. Why do you think Jesus and the New Testament spoke so often of hell?

4. "When love didn't compel me, fear corrected me. The thought of the workshop—and the weeping and gnashing of teeth therein—was just enough to straighten me out."

A. How is this kind of fear merely another face of love?

B. How does Max's personal experience relate to what God tells us of hell?

5. "People do not go to hell. Sinners do. The rebellious do. The

self-centered do. So how could a loving God send people to hell? He doesn't. He simply honors the choice of sinners."

    A. What do you think of Max's teaching above? Do you agree with him? Explain.

    B. If you have ever told a non-Christian something like this, what was the reaction? What happened?

LOOKING AHEAD

1. Read Revelation 9:20–21; 11:10; 14:9–11; 16:9–11, 21.

    A. How do the unredeemed react to God's judgments in these passages?

    B. How does God finally respond in Revelation 14:9–11?

2. Read Daniel 12:2 and Matthew 25:46.

    A. What two groups of people are mentioned in both of these texts?

    B. What are the respective destinies of these two groups?

    C. How long will these groups remain in their respective states?

3. Read Luke 16:19–31.

    A. What do you learn about hell in this passage?

    B. How do verses 27–28 show the insanity of saying, "I'll be OK in hell because that's where all my friends will be"?

4. Read Hebrews 2:14–18.

    A. Why did Jesus take on human flesh, according to this passage?

B. What did Jesus accomplish by his death, according to this passage?

C. What confidence can we have because Jesus did these things?

LOOKING IN

1. Although it will not be a pleasant study, get a concordance and look up all the verses it lists under the words *hell* or *Hades*. What do you discover in your study?

2. For one week, listen for the way people speak of the idea of "hell," whether at work, in the shopping mall, on TV, or in any movies you might see. What do people in this culture believe about hell? What phrases do they use that show an ignorance of its true nature? Why is this significant?

TWELVE

SEEING JESUS

LOOKING BACK

1. "Imagine God saying to you, 'I'll make a deal with you if you wish. I'll give you anything and everything you ask: pleasure, power, honor, wealth, freedom, even peace of mind and a good conscience. Nothing will be a sin; nothing will be forbidden; and nothing will be impossible to you. You will never be bored and you will never die. Only . . . you will never see my face.'"

A. How did you react when you first read this paragraph? Why?

B. How do you think your best friends would react if they were given this choice? Explain. How would you react? Explain.

2. "Paul doesn't measure the joy of encountering the apostles or embracing our loved ones. If we will be amazed at these, which certainly we will, he does not say. What he does say is that we will be amazed at Jesus."

A. Why will we be amazed at Jesus?

B. What amazes you about Jesus right now?

3. "The human tongue is inadequate to describe Christ. So in a breathless effort to tell us what he saw, John gives us symbols."

A. Why is the human tongue inadequate to describe Christ?

B. If you had to suggest some other symbols to describe Christ, what symbols might you choose? Describe and explain them.

4. Max describes Christ as:

- The Perfect Priest.
- The Only Pure One.
- The Source of Strength.
- The Sound of Love.
- The Everlasting Light.

A. Explain the significance of each of these descriptions.

B. Which of these descriptions means the most to you? Why?

LOOKING AHEAD

1. Read 1 John 3:1–3.

    A. How great is the love of God? What epitomizes that love, according to verse 1?

    B. What will happen when we see Christ, according to verse 2? Why will this happen?

    C. How is this knowledge supposed to affect us today, according to verse 3?

2. Read Revelation 1:10–18.

    A. What picture of Christ do you get when you read this passage? Explain.

    B. How did John react to this "unveiling" of Christ? Why was this appropriate?

    C. How did Jesus respond to John's reaction? How does this show us his astonishing love?

3. Read Zechariah 12:10–13:1.

    A. How does the prophet Zechariah picture the return of Christ?

    B. How does "the house of David" react to his coming?

    C. How does God respond in 13:1?

LOOKING IN

1. Memorize Hebrews 12:2–3. Meditate on this question: How can pondering Jesus keep you from growing weary and losing heart?

2. We live in a day in which differing views of Christ's coming have divided some Christians. How can you make sure that your own view does not add to this discord? How can it, in fact, encourage others and bring about peace and hope?

THIRTEEN

CROSSING THE THRESHOLD

LOOKING BACK

1. "Is she rebellious? Maybe. But mostly, she is just forgetful."

   A. How does the church sometimes "forget" about her fiancé, Christ?

   B. How can you make sure that you aren't one who forgets about Jesus?

2. "To forget the purpose of ginkgo is one thing. But to forget our engagement to Christ is another. We need a reminder! May I offer an incentive? *You have captured God's heart*."

   A. How do we know that we have "captured God's heart"?

B. How does it make you feel to know that you have captured God's heart?

C. How are we to respond to this wonderful knowledge?

3. "Allow his love to change the way you look at you."

A. How do you look at you right now?

B. How can Christ's love change the way you look at you?

4. "You might ask, 'Why hasn't he come?' There is only one answer. His bride is not ready. She is still being prepared."

A. How do you think the church is still being prepared for Christ?

B. In what ways is Christ preparing you for his return?

5. "We want to look our best for Christ. We want our hearts to be pure and our thoughts to be clean. We want our faces to shine with grace and our eyes to sparkle with love. We want to be prepared. Why? In hopes that he will love us? No. Just the opposite. Because he already does."

A. How does Christ's love for you cause you to seek personal purity?

B. What word do you think best describes Christ's love for you? Why this word?

LOOKING AHEAD

1. Read Ephesians 5:25–27.

A. What is Christ's vision for his church, according to these verses?

B. How do you "fit into" this vision? Does this description "fit" you? Explain.

2. Read Revelation 21:2, 9–27.

A. How does John picture "the bride of the Lamb"? What image comes to mind when you read this passage?

B. List the characteristics of the city you find in this passage. What do you think these varied characteristics are meant to teach us about this "bride"?

3. Read 2 Corinthians 11:2–3.

A. What was Paul's goal regarding the church at Corinth?

B. How ought this to be the goal of all of us?

C. How can we ensure that this goal is accomplished? What must we avoid?

4. Read Jeremiah 31:3; Isaiah 62:5; 1 John 4:10.

A. How does God feel about us, according to these passages?

B. How should we respond to this knowledge? How can we practically encourage ourselves to do this?

LOOKING IN

1. If you are married, get out your wedding album, sit down with your spouse, and reminisce over the day of your wedding. Then take a few moments to discuss "the marriage supper of the Lamb" described in Revelation 19:6–9. How will the wonderful feelings of your own marriage be multiplied and intensified on that day in heaven with Christ?

2. The next time you attend a wedding, prepare yourself by reading Revelation 19:6–9. How do human weddings preview the marriage supper of the Lamb? How can both encourage us in our walk of faith?

WITH AN EAR FOR THE TRUMPET

LOOKING BACK

1. "Like Fred, we took a fall. And, like Fred, we are trapped. Trapped, not by piano wires, but by guilt, anxiety, and pride."

   A. How do guilt, anxiety, and pride "trap" us?

   B. What kind of things tend to "trap" you? How can you be freed from them?

2. "God understands. And he gets creative. He coaxes. Through the fingers of circumstance and situation, he tries to get us to look up. But we, like Fred, make a dash for the corner."

   A. How has God been creative in your own experience to rescue you?

   B. In what ways do you "dash for the corner"? Why do you do this?

3. Max says we respond to God's overtures in several ways:

   • We pretend God doesn't exist.
   • We don't believe him.
   • We decide to give it a try.

A. Which of these responses have characterized you at some point in your life?

B. Which one, if any, characterizes you now? Explain.

4. "Fred finally made his way back to the place where he fell in. He looked up. And when he did, Sara was there. He lifted his head just high enough so that she could reach in and lift him out. Which is exactly what God will do for you. You will look up, and he will reach down and take you home . . . *when Christ comes.*"

A. What comes to mind when you think of the word *home*?

B. What are you most looking forward to about the day Christ comes?

Looking Ahead

1. Read Revelation 22:7, 12–14, 17, 20.

A. What does the apostle John emphasize in these final few verses?

B. What would you do today if you knew Christ were coming back at seven o'clock tonight?

2. Read 1 Thessalonians 4:16–18.

A. What three "sounds" are mentioned in this passage?

B. What will happen after we hear these sounds?

C. How does Paul expect that this truth will affect us right now?

3. Read Jude vs. 24–25.

A. How does Jude envision we will be presented to God?

B. Who is responsible for this great event?

C. What kind of response does this call forth from us?

4. Read 2 Peter 3:8–15.

A. How does Peter counsel us to counter thoughts that suggest Christ is not coming back?

B. What kind of people ought we to be, since Christ is coming back (vs. 11, 14)?

C. God's "patience" leads to what, according to verse 15?

Looking In

1. Memorize Jude vs. 24–25 and encourage a good friend or family member to memorize it with you. Then take some time and discuss how its truth can help you both grow in faith.

2. Regardless of the time of year, get out a good recording of Handel's *Messiah* and listen to the "Hallelujah Chorus"—and remind yourself that "the King of kings and Lord of lords" is coming back to this earth . . . for *you!*

The Lucado Reader's Guide

Discover . . . Inside every book by Max Lucado, you'll find words of encouragement and inspiration that will draw you into a deeper experience with Jesus and treasures for your walk with God. What will you discover?

3:16: The Numbers of Hope
. . . the 26 words that can change your life.
core scripture: John 3:16

And the Angels Were Silent
. . . what Jesus Christ's final days can teach you about what matters most.
core scripture: Matthew 20–27

The Applause of Heaven
. . . the secret to a truly satisfying life.
core scripture: The Beatitudes, Matthew 5:1–10

Come Thirsty
. . . how to rehydrate your heart and sink into the wellspring of God's love.
core scripture: John 7:37–38

Cure for the Common Life
. . . the unique things God designed you to do with your life.
core scripture: 1 Corinthians 12:7

Facing Your Giants
. . . when God is for you, no challenge is too great.
core scripture: 1 and 2 Samuel

Fearless
. . . how faith is the antidote to the fear in your life.
core scripture: John 14:1, 3

Grace
. . . the incredible gift that saves and sustains you.
core scripture: Hebrews 12:15

A Gentle Thunder
. . . the God who will do whatever it takes to lead his children back to him.
core scripture: Psalm 81:7

Great Day, Every Day
. . . how living in a purposeful way will help you trust more, stress less.
core scripture: Psalm 118:24

The Great House of God
. . . a blueprint for peace, joy, and love found in the Lord's Prayer.
core scripture: The Lord's Prayer, Matthew 6:9–13

God Came Near
. . . a love so great that it left heaven to become part of your world.
core scripture: John 1:14

He Chose the Nails
. . . a love so deep that it chose death on a cross—just to win your heart.
core scripture: 1 Peter 1:18–20

He Still Moves Stones
. . . the God who still does the impossible—in your life.
core scripture: Matthew 12:20

In the Eye of the Storm
. . . peace in the storms of your life.
core scripture: John 6

In the Grip of Grace
. . . the greatest gift of all—the grace of God.
core scripture: Romans

It's Not About Me
. . . why focusing on God will make sense of your life.
core scripture: 2 Corinthians 3:18

Just Like Jesus
. . . a life free from guilt, fear, and anxiety.
core scripture: Ephesians 4:23–24

A Love Worth Giving
. . . how living loved frees you to love others.
core scripture: 1 Corinthians 13

Next Door Savior
. . . a God who walked life's hardest trials—and still walks with you through yours.
core scripture: Matthew 16:13–16

No Wonder They Call Him the Savior
. . . hope in the unlikeliest place—upon the cross.
core scripture: Romans 5:15

Outlive Your Life
. . . that a great God created you to do great things.
core scripture: Acts 1

Six Hours One Friday
. . . forgiveness and healing in the middle of loss and failure.
core scripture: John 19–20

Traveling Light
. . . the power to release the burdens you were never meant to carry.
core scripture: Psalm 23

When God Whispers Your Name
. . . the path to hope in knowing that God knows you, never forgets you, and cares about the details of your life.
core scripture: John 10:3

When Christ Comes
. . . why the best is yet to come.
core scripture: 1 Corinthians 15:23

You'll Get Through This
. . . hope in the midst of your hard times and a God who uses the mess of life for good.
core scripture: Genesis 50:20

Recommended reading if you're struggling with . . .

FEAR AND WORRY

Come Thirsty
Fearless
For the Tough Times
Next Door Savior
Traveling Light

DISCOURAGEMENT

He Still Moves Stones
Next Door Savior

GRIEF/DEATH OF A LOVED ONE

Next Door Savior
Traveling Light
When Christ Comes
When God Whispers Your Name
You'll Get Through This

GUILT

In the Grip of Grace
Just Like Jesus

LONELINESS

God Came Near

SIN

Facing Your Giants
He Chose the Nails
Six Hours One Friday

WEARINESS

When God Whispers Your Name
You'll Get Through This

Recommended reading if you want to know more about . . .

THE CROSS

And the Angels Were Silent
He Chose the Nails
No Wonder They Call Him the Savior
Six Hours One Friday

GRACE

Grace
He Chose the Nails
In the Grip of Grace

HEAVEN

The Applause of Heaven
When Christ Comes

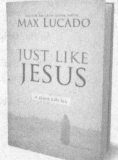

SHARING THE GOSPEL

God Came Near
Grace
No Wonder They Call Him the Savior

Recommended reading if you're looking for more . . .

COMFORT
For the Tough Times
He Chose the Nails
Next Door Savior
Traveling Light
You'll Get Through This

COMPASSION
Outlive Your Life

COURAGE
Facing Your Giants
Fearless

HOPE
3:16: The Numbers of Hope
Facing Your Giants
A Gentle Thunder
God Came Near
Grace

JOY
The Applause of Heaven
Cure for the Common Life
When God Whispers Your Name

LOVE
Come Thirsty
A Love Worth Giving
No Wonder They Call Him the Savior

PEACE
And the Angels Were Silent
The Great House of God
In the Eye of the Storm
Traveling Light
You'll Get Through This

SATISFACTION
And the Angels Were Silent
Come Thirsty
Cure for the Common Life
Great Day Every Day

TRUST
A Gentle Thunder
It's Not About Me
Next Door Savior

Max Lucado books make great gifts!
If you're coming up to a special occasion, consider one of these.

FOR ADULTS:
For the Tough Times
Grace for the Moment
Live Loved
The Lucado Life Lessons Study Bible
Mocha with Max
DaySpring Daybrighteners® and cards

FOR TEENS/GRADUATES:
Let the Journey Begin
You Can Be Everything God Wants You to Be
You Were Made to Make a Difference

FOR KIDS:
Just in Case You Ever Wonder
The Oak Inside the Acorn
You Are Special

FOR PASTORS AND TEACHERS:
God Thinks You're Wonderful
You Changed My Life

AT CHRISTMAS:
The Crippled Lamb
Christmas Stories from Max Lucado
God Came Near

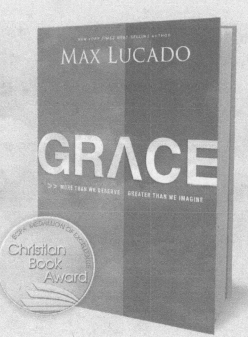

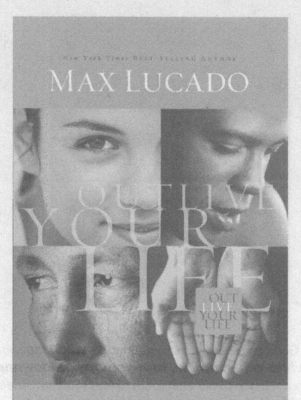

Inspired by what you just read?
Connect with Max.

Hope . Pure and simple .

Listen to Max's teaching ministry, UpWords, on the radio and online. Visit www.MaxLucado.com to get FREE resources for spiritual growth and encouragement, including:

- Archives of UpWords, Max's daily radio program, and a list of radio stations where it airs
- Devotionals and e-mails from Max
- First look at book excerpts
- Downloads of audio, video, and printed material
- Mobile content

You will also find an online store and special offers.

www.MaxLucado.com
1-800-822-9673

UpWords Ministries
P.O. Box 692170
San Antonio, TX 78269-2170

Join the Max Lucado community:

Follow Max on Twitter @MaxLucado
or at Facebook.com/MaxLucado